CODING INTERVIEW NINJA

HOW TO CRUSH YOUR CODING INTERVIEWS AND LAND YOUR DREAM JOB

RAHUL LAHORIA

Made with ♥ on the Notion Press Platform
www.notionpress.com

I would like to express my deepest gratitude and appreciation to my family and friends who have stood by me through thick and thin. Without their unwavering support and encouragement, I would not have been able to embark on this journey of writing a book.

To my family, thank you for being my pillars of strength, for believing in me and for always inspiring me to pursue my passions. You have been my constant source of motivation and your unwavering love has sustained me through the ups and downs of life.

To my teachers, mentors and guides, I am deeply grateful for your guidance and mentorship. You have taught me valuable lessons and shaped my thinking and approach towards life. Your invaluable support and encouragement have helped me in achieving my dreams and reaching my full potential.

To my readers, it is my sincere hope that the knowledge and insights shared in this book will help you in achieving your goals. I hope this book will serve as a guide and inspire you to reach your full potential.

Last but not least, I would like to dedicate this book to all those who have helped and supported me throughout this journey. Your belief in me has been a constant source of inspiration and motivation. Thank you for being an integral part of my life and for making me who I am today.

-- Rahul Lahoria

Contents

Contents

Contents

Foreword

Landing a job in the tech industry can be a daunting task, especially if you're just starting out or transitioning from a different career path. As someone who has gone through the process myself and has interviewed hundreds of candidates, I can tell you that the competition is fierce and the expectations are high.

However, there is a way to stand out from the crowd and increase your chances of success: by becoming a coding interview ninja. In this book, you'll learn the strategies, techniques, and best practices that will help you crush your coding interviews and land your dream job.

The book is divided into three parts, each focusing on a different phase of the interview process: Preparation, Publishing, and Performing. In the Preparation phase, you'll discover how to build a strong foundation of technical knowledge, sharpen your problem-solving skills, and improve your communication and presentation skills.

In the Publishing phase, you'll learn how to find the right companies to apply to, optimize your resume and online presence, and network effectively to increase your visibility and referrals.

Finally, in the Performing phase, you'll discover how to ace different types of coding interviews, including phone screens, coding challenges, whiteboard sessions, and behavioral interviews. You'll also learn how to negotiate job offers, navigate the onboarding process, and set yourself up for long-term success.

Throughout the book, you'll find practical tips, real-world examples, and exercises that will help you apply the concepts to your own situation. Whether you're a recent graduate, a career changer, or a seasoned professional, Coding Interview Ninja will provide you with the tools and confidence you need to succeed in the competitive world of tech.

I highly recommend this book to anyone who is serious about landing their dream job in the tech industry. Good luck on your journey, and remember: with the right mindset, preparation, and practice, you can become a coding interview ninja too.

Best regards,

Rajnish Kumar

Preface

Have you ever applied for a job in the tech industry and felt overwhelmed by the coding interview process? Have you struggled to answer technical questions on the spot, or found it challenging to communicate your ideas effectively? Have you wondered how to stand out from the competition and secure your dream job?

If you answered yes to any of these questions, you're not alone. Landing a job in the tech industry can be a challenging and competitive process, especially if you're new to the field or looking to make a transition. As a hiring manager and technical interviewer, I've seen countless candidates struggle with the same issues, even those who have years of experience under their belts.

That's why I wrote this book. Drawing from my own experience as a software engineer, technical interviewer, and hiring manager, as well as from the insights and feedback of other tech professionals, I've put together a comprehensive guide to help you succeed in the coding interview process and land your dream job.

This book is designed to be a practical and actionable resource that covers every aspect of the coding interview process, from preparing for the interview to performing at your best on interview day. You'll learn how to build a strong technical foundation, sharpen your problem-solving and communication skills, and navigate the interview process with confidence and ease.

The book is divided into three parts. In the first part, Preparation, you'll learn how to build your technical knowledge, practice your problem-solving skills, and improve your communication and presentation skills. In the second part, Publishing, you'll discover how to find the right companies to apply to, optimize your resume and online presence, and network effectively to increase your visibility and referrals. Finally, in the third part, Performing, you'll learn how to ace different types of coding interviews, including phone screens, coding challenges, whiteboard sessions, and behavioral interviews.

Each chapter includes practical tips, real-world examples, and exercises that will help you apply the concepts to your own situation. Whether you're a recent graduate, a career changer, or a seasoned professional, Coding Interview Ninja will provide you with the tools and confidence you need to succeed in the competitive world of tech.

I hope you find this book helpful on your journey to becoming a coding interview ninja. Remember that landing your dream job is not just about technical skills, but also about your mindset, preparation, and practice. With the right approach and determination, you can crush your coding interviews and achieve your career goals.

Good luck, and happy interviewing!

Rahul Lahoria

Acknowledgements

I would like to express my heartfelt gratitude to all those who have supported me throughout my journey of writing this book.

First and foremost, I want to thank my wife Mamta for her unwavering support, encouragement, and patience throughout this process. Her constant motivation and feedback have been invaluable in bringing this book to life.

I would also like to extend my deepest appreciation to my parents, Shamsher Singh and Maya Devi, for their unconditional love and support. Their unwavering belief in me and their constant encouragement have been a driving force behind my success.

I would like to express my sincere gratitude to all the individuals who have been instrumental in shaping my knowledge and understanding in the field of software development. My teachers, mentors, and colleagues have all played a significant role in shaping my thought process and inspiring me to pursue my passion for coding.

I am also grateful to my publisher for their guidance, support, and commitment to making this book a success. Their expertise and professionalism have been invaluable in bringing this project to fruition

Lastly, I would like to thank my readers for their time and interest in this book. I hope that the information shared in these pages proves to be beneficial in achieving your goals and aspirations.

Thank you all for your contributions and support.

Prologue

It was the day of my first coding interview. I had spent weeks preparing, studying algorithms and data structures, practicing coding challenges, and rehearsing my elevator pitch. I had read every article and watched every video on how to ace the coding interview, and I felt confident that I was ready for whatever the interviewers would throw at me.

Or so I thought.

As soon as the interview started, my confidence began to waver. The questions were not what I had expected, and my mind went blank. I struggled to come up with a solution, and even when I did, I had a hard time explaining my thought process. The interviewers seemed unimpressed, and I left the interview feeling defeated and discouraged.

Over the next few weeks, I received several more rejections and realized that I needed to rethink my approach. I started talking to other tech professionals, both on the hiring side and on the candidate side, and discovered that I was not alone in my struggles. Many people had faced similar challenges in the coding interview process, and many had found ways to overcome them.

That's when I decided to write this book. I wanted to share my own experiences and insights, as well as those of other tech professionals, and provide a practical and actionable guide to help others succeed in the coding interview process.

Whether you're just starting out in your tech career or looking to make a transition, this book is for you. It covers everything from technical knowledge to communication and presentation skills, from networking to job search strategies, and from coding challenges to behavioral interviews. It's designed to be a comprehensive and practical resource that will help you become a coding interview ninja and land your dream job.

I hope this book will help you on your journey to success and that you'll find it both informative and enjoyable to read.

Remember that the coding interview process is not easy, but with the right mindset, preparation, and practice, you can overcome any challenge and achieve your career goals.

Let's get started!

Rahul Lahoria

1st P : Prepare (What your should learn for a coding Interview?)

Preparation is the key to success, and a comprehensive guide can be your greatest ally in unlocking your potential and achieving your goals

CHAPTER ONE

The Turning Point

I remember the day like it was yesterday. It was 28th October 2013, and I was in my semi-final semester of college. At the time, I had big plans to start my own company once I finished my degree. But as fate would have it, that plan was put on hold when I received a call from my father that would change everything.

I was riding my bicycle back to my hostel room after a day in the lab when my phone began to ring. I stopped and checked the caller ID. It was my father. I greeted him with a "Namaste Daddy, how are you?" But his voice was shaking, and I knew something was wrong.

He explained to me that we had a family problem that required 5 lakh rupees to be resolved within the next six months. For me, this was a huge amount of money, and I knew there was no way I could help out without finding a job first.

The only option for me was to try and get a job. The problem was, I only had one month to prepare for the companies that were coming to IIT Kharagpur in December. My friends, who had been preparing for the job for the past six months, were way ahead of me.

It seemed impossible to cover all the topics in computer science in such a short time. There were more than 40 subjects to cover, and even the GATE exam had 13 subjects. I felt like I was losing hope with each passing day.

But then, something within me snapped, and I decided to take matters into my own hands. I started researching, trying to figure out what it really took to win a coding interview. I scoured the internet, read books, and talked to professors and alumni seniors, all in an effort to figure out what I needed to do.

After a lot of hard work, I finally came to the realization that there were three key subjects that I needed to master in order to win a coding interview. First, I needed to know a stack. This could be a mean stack, mern stack, php or python. Second, I needed to have a deep understanding of data structures and algorithms. Finally, I needed to know database and management systems.

With this newfound knowledge, I buckled down and studied harder than I ever had before. I poured over textbooks, online courses, and took practice exams until my eyes hurt. But slowly and surely, I began to see progress.

As the day of the interviews approached, I was filled with nervous excitement. But when the day finally arrived, I walked into that interview room with a newfound confidence. I knew that I had prepared as much as I possibly could, and that I was as ready as I could be.

And when the results came back, I was thrilled to find out that I had landed a job! It was a dream come true, and I knew that I had achieved something that I never thought was possible.

From that day on, I realized that anything was possible if I put in the hard work and dedication needed to achieve my goals. And while my journey to success was far from easy, it taught me that with perseverance and a willingness to learn, anything is possible.

CHAPTER TWO

Mastering Data Structures and Algorithms: Essential Concepts for Programming Success

As students of computer science, you must be familiar with the term "data structures and algorithms". It is a crucial part of computer science that is necessary to understand if you want to become a good programmer. You might think that it is a vast topic, but if you see closely, there are not more than 50 coding problems that you need to understand.

Let's start by talking about data structures. There are seven data structures that you should know, namely array, string, linked list, stack, queue, tree, and graph. You should know how to put an element inside these data structures, how to retrieve an element, remove an element, search an element, and update an element. Once you understand these data structures, it will be easier for you to solve complex problems in programming.

Next, we move on to searching and sorting algorithms. In searching algorithms, you have two options- linear search and binary search. In sorting algorithms, you have bubble sort, selection sort, insertion sort, quick sort, merge sort, and heap sort. It is essential to know the time and space complexity of these algorithms. You must know the worst-case time complexity, average time complexity, and best time complexity of each algorithm. It will help you to choose the best algorithm for a particular problem.

The last part of our discussion is design paradigms. There are four design paradigms- divide and conquer, greedy programming, dynamic programming, and backtracking. You must know at least three examples from each design pattern. For example, binary search, quick sort, and merge sort are the examples of the divide and conquer paradigm.

Now, you might be wondering why it is essential to learn all these things. Let me tell you that understanding data structures and algorithms is crucial to becoming a good programmer. It will help you to solve complex problems and write efficient code. It will also help you to understand and analyze the existing code.

When you start learning data structures and algorithms, start by understanding the basics of each data structure and algorithm. Don't try to rush things as it is a vast topic. Take your time and go through each topic step by step. Try to implement the code yourself and solve coding problems. You can use online resources, books, and courses to learn these topics.

Another essential thing to keep in mind is to practice regularly. Don't just read and forget. Practice coding problems regularly to sharpen your skills. Try to participate in coding competitions and hackathons to challenge yourself.

In conclusion, data structures and algorithms are an essential part of computer science that you must learn if you want to become a good programmer. You need to understand the basics of each data structure and algorithm, along with their time and space complexity. You should also know the design paradigms and examples of each paradigm. So, keep learning and practicing to become a skilled programmer.

CHAPTER THREE

Data Structure and Algorithms: In Need of Your Focus

Data structures are an essential part of computer science and programming. They are the backbone of all kinds of algorithms and software systems. In this article, we will explore the different types of data structures.

1. **Arrays:**

   Arrays are one of the most basic data structures in computer programming. An array is a collection of elements of the same data type, which are stored in contiguous memory locations. The elements in an array are accessed using an index, which starts from 0.

2. **Linked Lists:**

   A linked list is a collection of nodes, where each node contains a value and a pointer to the next node in the list. Linked lists can be singly linked, where each node has only a next pointer, or doubly linked, where each node has both a next and a previous pointer.

3. **Stacks:**

   A stack is a linear data structure that follows the Last In First Out (LIFO) principle. It is a collection of elements that supports two main operations: push and pop. The push operation adds an element to the top of the stack, while the pop operation removes the top element from the stack.

4. **Queues:**

   A queue is a linear data structure that follows the First In First Out (FIFO) principle. It is a collection of elements that supports two main operations: enqueue and dequeue. The enqueue operation adds an element to the end of the queue, while the dequeue operation removes the front element from the queue.

5. **Trees:**

   A tree is a hierarchical data structure consisting of nodes connected by edges. The topmost node is called the root node, and each node can have any number of children nodes. Trees can be binary, where each node has at most two children, or n-ary, where each node can have any number of children.

6. **Graphs:**

   A graph is a non-linear data structure consisting of nodes connected by edges. Unlike trees, graphs can have cycles and can be directed or undirected. Graphs are used to represent complex relationships and networks, such as social networks and road networks.

7. **Hash Tables:**

A hash table is a data structure that allows quick access to data based on a key. It is implemented using an array and a hash function, which maps keys to array indices. Hash tables have constant-time access to elements and are used for fast lookups and indexing.

8. **Heaps:**

   A heap is a binary tree-based data structure that satisfies the heap property, which means that each node is greater than or equal to its parent node. Heaps are used to implement priority queues, where elements with higher priorities are dequeued before elements with lower priorities.

In conclusion, data structures are fundamental building blocks of computer programs, and each type of data structure has its own unique properties and applications. Understanding the different types of data structures is crucial for any programmer to be able to choose the right data structure for the job and write efficient and scalable code.

Algorithmic Alchemy: The Art of Designing Efficient Solutions for Coding Interviews

As a fresher, you should focus on having a basic understanding of all the algorithm design paradigms, including Divide and Conquer, Greedy, Dynamic Programming, Backtracking, and Brute Force.

Here are brief definitions and examples of each paradigm:

1. **Divide and Conquer:**

   Divide and Conquer is an algorithm design paradigm in which

a problem is broken down into smaller sub-problems that are solved recursively. The solutions of the sub-problems are combined to solve the original problem. Examples of Divide and Conquer algorithms are Quick Sort, Merge Sort, and Binary Search.

2. **Greedy:**

   Greedy algorithms make locally optimal choices at each step, with the hope of finding a global optimum solution. The algorithm makes the choice that seems to be the best at that moment and solves the sub-problems, which arise after the choice. Examples of Greedy algorithms are Kruskal's algorithm for finding the Minimum Spanning Tree, Dijkstra's algorithm for finding the Shortest Path, and Huffman Encoding.

3. **Dynamic Programming:**

   Dynamic Programming is a programming paradigm used to solve optimization problems by breaking them down into simpler sub-problems and storing the results of each sub-problem to avoid repetitive computations. Examples of Dynamic Programming algorithms are the Longest Common Subsequence problem, the Knapsack problem, and the Fibonacci sequence.

4. **Backtracking**:

   Backtracking is a general algorithmic technique that involves trying out all possible solutions and then selecting the one that works. It is used for problems where the solution is a sequence of choices, each leading to a sub-problem until a solution is found. Examples of Backtracking algorithms are the N-Queens problem, Sudoku, and the Hamiltonian Cycle problem.

5. **Brute Force:**

   Brute Force is a straightforward approach to solving a problem, which involves trying out all possible solutions to find the best one. This approach is usually very time-consuming and inefficient for larger problems. Examples of Brute Force algorithms are the Traveling Salesman problem, the Subset Sum problem, and the Maximum Subarray problem.

As a fresher, it's essential to have a basic understanding of all these paradigms and their respective algorithms.

The key operations of Arrays in JavaScript with example code for each operation:

1. **Declaring an array:**

   To declare an array in JavaScript, you use the square brackets [ ]. Here's an example code:

```
const arr = []; // declaring an empty array
```

Declaring an array

2. **Initializing an array:**

   To initialize an array in JavaScript, you can assign values to the elements of the array using the square brackets and comma-separated values. Here's an example code:

```
const arr = [10, 20, 30, 40, 50]; // initializing an array of integers
```

Initializing an array

3. **Accessing array elements:**

   To access the elements of an array in JavaScript, you use the index inside the square brackets. Here's an example code:

```
const arr = [10, 20, 30, 40, 50];
console.log(arr[2]); // accessing the third element of the array
```

Accessing array elements

   Output: 30

4. **Iterating over array elements:**

   To iterate over the elements of an array in JavaScript, you can use a for loop that iterates over the array indices. Here's an example code:

```
const arr = [10, 20, 30, 40, 50];
for (let i = 0; i < arr.length; i++) {
    console.log(arr[i]); // printing each element of the array
}
```

Iterating over array elements

   Output: 10 20 30 40 50

5. **Changing the value of an array element:**

   To change the value of an element in an array in JavaScript, you can use the index inside the square brackets to access the element and then assign a new value to it. Here's an example code:

```
const arr = [10, 20, 30, 40, 50];
arr[2] = 35; // changing the value of the third element of the array
console.log(arr[2]); // accessing the new value of the third element
```

Changing the value of an array elemen

Output: 35

6. **Finding the length of an array:**

To find the length of an array in JavaScript, you can use the length property of the array. Here's an example code:

```
const arr = [10, 20, 30, 40, 50];
const len = arr.length; // finding the length of the array
console.log(len); // printing the length of the array
```

Finding the length of an array

Output: 5

7. Sorting an array:

To sort an array in JavaScript, you can use the sort method of the array. Here's an example code:

```
const arr = [50, 10, 40, 20, 30];
arr.sort(); // sorting the array in ascending order
console.log(arr); // printing the sorted array
```

Sorting an array

Output: 10 20 30 40 50

These are some of the key operations of arrays in JavaScript, but there are many more operations that you can perform on arrays depending on your requirements.

The key operations of Strings in JavaScript with example code for each operation:

1. **Declaring a string:**

   To declare a string in JavaScript, you can use single quotes or double quotes. Here's an example code:

```
const str = 'Hello, world!'; // declaring a string using single quotes
const str2 = "Hello, world!"; // declaring a string using double quotes
```

Declaring a string

2. **Accessing string characters:**

   To access individual characters in a string in JavaScript, you can use square brackets and the index of the character. Here's an example code:

```
const str = 'Hello, world!';
console.log(str[0]); // accessing the first character of the string
console.log(str[7]); // accessing the eighth character of the string
```

Accessing string characters

Output: H w

3. **Concatenating strings:**

   To concatenate two or more strings in JavaScript, you can use the + operator or the concat method. Here's an example code:

```
const str1 = 'Hello,';
const str2 = 'world!';
const str3 = str1 + ' ' + str2; // concatenating two strings using the + op
const str4 = str1.concat(' ', str2); // concatenating two strings using the
console.log(str3); // printing the concatenated string
console.log(str4); // printing the concatenated string
```

Concatenating strings

Output: Hello, world! Hello, world!

4. **Finding the length of a string:**

   To find the length of a string in JavaScript, you can use the length property. Here's an example code:

```
const str = 'Hello, world!';
console.log(str.length); // finding the length of the string
```

Finding the length of a string

Output: 13

5. **Searching for a substring:**

   To search for a substring in a string in JavaScript, you can use the indexOf or includes method. Here's an example code:

```
const str = 'Hello, world!';
console.log(str.indexOf('world')); // finding the index of the first occurr
console.log(str.includes('world')); // checking if the substring exists in
```

Searching for a substring

Output: 7 true

The key operations of linked lists in JavaScript with example code for each operation:

1. **Declaring a linked list:**

   To declare a linked list in JavaScript, you can define a Node class that contains a value property and a next property that points to the next node in the list. Here's an example code:

```
class Node {
  constructor(value) {
    this.value = value;
    this.next = null;
  }
}

class LinkedList {
  constructor() {
    this.head = null;
    this.tail = null;
    this.length = 0;
  }
}
```

Declaring a linked list

2. **Adding a node to the linked list:**

   To add a node to the linked list, you can define a add method that creates a new node and sets the next property of the last node in the list to point to the new node. Here's an example code:

```
class LinkedList {
  constructor() {
    this.head = null;
    this.tail = null;
    this.length = 0;
  }

  add(value) {
    const node = new Node(value);
    if (!this.head) {
      this.head = node;
      this.tail = node;
    } else {
      this.tail.next = node;
      this.tail = node;
    }
    this.length++;
  }
}

const list = new LinkedList();
list.add(1);
list.add(2);
list.add(3);
console.log(list); // { head: { value: 1, next: { value: 2, next: { value:
```

Adding a node to the linked list

3. **Removing a node from the linked list:**

   To remove a node from the linked list, you can define a remove method that finds the node with the specified value and removes it by setting the next property of the previous node to point to the next node. Here's an example code:

```
class LinkedList {
  constructor() {
    this.head = null;
    this.tail = null;
    this.length = 0;
  }

  add(value) {
    // ...
  }

  remove(value) {
    let current = this.head;
    let previous = null;
    while (current) {
      if (current.value === value) {
        if (!previous) {
          this.head = current.next;
        } else {
          previous.next = current.next;
        }
        if (current === this.tail) {
          this.tail = previous;
        }
        this.length--;
        break;
      }
      previous = current;
      current = current.next;
    }
  }
}

const list = new LinkedList();
list.add(1);
list.add(2);
list.add(3);
list.remove(2);
console.log(list); // { head: { value: 1, next: { value: 3, next: null } },
```

Removing a node from the linked list

4. **Finding a node in the linked list:**

   To find a node in the linked list, you can define a find method that iterates through the list and returns the node with the specified value. Here's an example code:

```
class LinkedList {
  constructor() {
    this.head = null;
    this.tail = null;
    this.length = 0;
  }

  add(value) {
    // ...
  }

  remove(value) {
    // ...
  }

  find(value) {
    let current = this.head;
    while (current) {
      if (current.value === value) {
        return current;
      }
      current = current.next;
    }
```

Finding a node in the linked list

The key operations of Stacks in JavaScript with example code for each operation:

1. **Declaring a stack:**

   To declare a stack in JavaScript, you can define an array and initialize it to an empty array. Here's an example code:

```
const stack = [];
```

Declaring a stack

2. **Adding an element to the top of the stack:**

   To add an element to the top of the stack, you can use the push method of the array. Here's an example code:

```
stack.push(1);
stack.push(2);
stack.push(3);
console.log(stack); // [1, 2, 3]
```

Adding an element to the top of the stack

3. **Removing an element from the top of the stack:**

   To remove an element from the top of the stack, you can use the pop method of the array. Here's an example code:

```
stack.pop();
console.log(stack); // [1, 2]
```

Removing an element from the top of the stack

4. **Retrieving the element at the top of the stack:**

   To retrieve the element at the top of the stack, you can use the slice method of the array. Here's an example code:

```
const top = stack.slice(-1)[0];
console.log(top); // 2
```

Retrieving the element at the top of the stack

The key operations of queues in JavaScript with example code for each operation:

1. **Declaring a queue:**

   To declare a queue in JavaScript, you can define an array and initialize it to an empty array. Here's an example code:

```
const queue = [];
```

Declaring a queue

2. **Adding an element to the back of the queue:**

   To add an element to the back of the queue, you can use the push method of the array. Here's an example code:

```
queue.push(1);
queue.push(2);
queue.push(3);
console.log(queue); // [1, 2, 3]
```

Adding an element to the back of the queue

3. **Removing an element from the front of the queue:**

   To remove an element from the front of the queue, you can use the shift method of the array. Here's an example code:

```
queue.shift();
console.log(queue); // [2, 3]
```

Enter Caption

4. **Retrieving the element at the front of the queue:**

   To retrieve the element at the front of the queue, you can use the slice method of the array. Here's an example code:

```
const front = queue.slice(0, 1)[0];
console.log(front); // 2
```

Retrieving the element at the front of the queue

5. **Checking if the queue is empty:**

   To check if the queue is empty, you can use the length property of the array. Here's an example code:

```
if (queue.length === 0) {
  console.log("Queue is empty");
} else {
  console.log("Queue is not empty");
}
```

Checking if the queue is empty

The key operations of Trees in JavaScript with example code for each operation:

1. **Creating a tree:**

   To create a tree in JavaScript, you can define a constructor function for the tree and use the new operator to create a new instance of the tree. Here's an example code:

```
function TreeNode(val) {
  this.val = val;
  this.left = null;
  this.right = null;
}

const root = new TreeNode(1);
root.left = new TreeNode(2);
root.right = new TreeNode(3);
root.left.left = new TreeNode(4);
root.left.right = new TreeNode(5);
console.log(root);
```

Creating a tree

2. **Traversing the tree:**

   There are several ways to traverse a tree, including inorder traversal, preorder traversal, and postorder traversal. Here's an example code for inorder traversal:

```
function inorderTraversal(root) {
  if (!root) return [];
  const result = [];
  function inorder(node) {
    if (!node) return;
    inorder(node.left);
    result.push(node.val);
    inorder(node.right);
  }
  inorder(root);
  return result;
}

console.log(inorderTraversal(root)); // [4, 2, 5, 1, 3]
```

Enter Caption

3. **Searching for a value in the tree:**

   To search for a value in the tree, you can use a recursive function to traverse the tree and check if each node matches the target value. Here's an example code:

```
function search(root, target) {
  if (!root) return false;
  if (root.val === target) return true;
  return search(root.left, target) || search(root.right, target);
}

console.log(search(root, 3)); // true
console.log(search(root, 6)); // false
```

Searching for a value in the tree

4. **Adding a node to the tree:**

   To add a node to the tree, you can use a recursive function to find the appropriate position for the new node and insert it there. Here's an example code:

```
function insert(root, val) {
  if (!root) return new TreeNode(val);
  if (val < root.val) {
    root.left = insert(root.left, val);
  } else {
    root.right = insert(root.right, val);
  }
  return root;
}

insert(root, 6);
console.log(root); // the tree now has a new node with value 6
```

Adding a node to the tree

5. **Removing a node from the tree:**

   To remove a node from the tree, you can use a recursive function to find the node to be removed and replace it with the appropriate successor or predecessor node. Here's an example code:

```
function remove(root, target) {
  if (!root) return null;
  if (target < root.val) {
    root.left = remove(root.left, target);
  } else if (target > root.val) {
    root.right = remove(root.right, target);
  } else {
    if (!root.left) return root.right;
    if (!root.right) return root.left;
    let temp = root.right;
    while (temp.left) {
      temp = temp.left;
    }
    root.val = temp.val;
    root.right = remove(root.right, temp.val);
  }
  return root;
}

remove(root, 5);
console.log(root); // the tree now has node with value 5 removed
```

Removing a node from the tree

the key operations of graphs in JavaScript with example code for each operation:

1. **Creating a graph:**

   To create a graph in JavaScript, you can define a constructor function for the graph and use the new operator to create a new instance of the graph. Here's an example code:

```
function Graph() {
  this.vertices = [];
  this.edges = {};
}

Graph.prototype.addVertex = function(vertex) {
  this.vertices.push(vertex);
  this.edges[vertex] = [];
};

Graph.prototype.addEdge = function(vertex1, vertex2) {
  this.edges[vertex1].push(vertex2);
  this.edges[vertex2].push(vertex1);
};

const g = new Graph();
g.addVertex('A');
g.addVertex('B');
g.addVertex('C');
g.addEdge('A', 'B');
g.addEdge('B', 'C');
console.log(g.vertices); // ['A', 'B', 'C']
console.log(g.edges); // { A: ['B'], B: ['A', 'C'], C: ['B'] }
```

Creating a graph

2. **Traversing the graph:**

   There are several ways to traverse a graph, including depth-first search and breadth-first search. Here's an example code for depth-first search:

```
Graph.prototype.dfs = function(vertex, visited = new Set(), result = []) {
  visited.add(vertex);
  result.push(vertex);
  for (let neighbor of this.edges[vertex]) {
    if (!visited.has(neighbor)) {
      this.dfs(neighbor, visited, result);
    }
  }
  return result;
};

console.log(g.dfs('A')); // ['A', 'B', 'C']
```

Traversing the graph

3. **Searching for a value in the graph:**

   To search for a value in the graph, you can use a recursive function to traverse the graph and check if each vertex matches the target value. Here's an example code:

```
Graph.prototype.search = function(vertex, target, visited = new Set()) {
  visited.add(vertex);
  if (vertex === target) return true;
  for (let neighbor of this.edges[vertex]) {
    if (!visited.has(neighbor)) {
      if (this.search(neighbor, target, visited)) {
        return true;
      }
    }
  }
  return false;
};

console.log(g.search('A', 'C')); // true
console.log(g.search('C', 'A')); // false
```

Searching for a value in the graph

4. **Adding a vertex to the graph:**

   To add a vertex to the graph, you can simply push the new vertex to the vertices array and add an empty array for the new vertex in the edges object. Here's an example code:

```
Graph.prototype.addVertex = function(vertex) {
  this.vertices.push(vertex);
  this.edges[vertex] = [];
};

g.addVertex('D');
console.log(g.vertices); // ['A', 'B', 'C', 'D']
console.log(g.edges); // { A: ['B'], B: ['A', 'C'], C: ['B'], D: [] }
```

Adding a vertex to the graph

5. **Removing a vertex from the graph:**

   To remove a vertex from the graph, you can remove the vertex from the vertices array and delete the corresponding array in the edges object. You also need to remove all edges that are connected to the vertex being removed. Here's an example code:

```
Graph.prototype.removeVertex = function(vertex) {
  this.vertices = this.vertices.filter(v => v !== vertex);
  delete this.edges[vertex];
  for (let v of this.vertices) {
    this.edges[v] = this.edges[v].filter(n => n !== vertex);
  }
};

g.removeVertex('C');
console.log(g.vertices); // ['A',
```

Removing a vertex from the graph

The key operations of Hash Tables in JavaScript with example code for each operation:

1. **Creating a hash table:**

   To create a hash table in JavaScript, you can use an object literal to define the table and its initial properties. Here's an example code:

```
const table = {
  'Alice': 25,
  'Bob': 30,
  'Charlie': 35,
};
```

Creating a hash table

2. Adding a key-value pair to the hash table:

   To add a new key-value pair to the hash table, you can simply use the key to assign a value to the table object. Here's an example code:

```
table['David'] = 40;
console.log(table); // { 'Alice': 25, 'Bob': 30, 'Charlie': 35, 'David': 40
```

Adding a key-value pair to the hash table

3. **Retrieving a value from the hash table:**

   To retrieve a value from the hash table, you can use the key to access the corresponding value in the table object. Here's an example code:

```
console.log(table['Bob']); // 30
```

Retrieving a value from the hash table:

4. **Updating a value in the hash table:**

   To update a value in the hash table, you can use the key to reassign a new value to the table object. Here's an example code:

```
table['Charlie'] = 36;
console.log(table); // { 'Alice': 25, 'Bob': 30, 'Charlie': 36, 'David': 40
```

Updating a value in the hash table

5. **Deleting a key-value pair from the hash table:**

   To delete a key-value pair from the hash table, you can use the delete keyword to remove the key and its corresponding value from the table object. Here's an example code:

```
delete table['Bob'];
console.log(table); // { 'Alice': 25, 'Charlie': 36, 'David': 40 }
```

Deleting a key-value pair from the hash table

6. **Handling collisions in hash tables:**

To handle collisions in hash tables, you can use a technique called separate chaining, where each key-value pair is stored in a linked list at the corresponding hash index. Here's an example code:

```
function HashTable() {
  this.table = new Array(137);
}

HashTable.prototype.hash = function(key) {
  let total = 0;
  for (let i = 0; i < key.length; i++) {
    total += key.charCodeAt(i);
  }
  return total % this.table.length;
};

HashTable.prototype.put = function(key, value) {
  const index = this.hash(key);
  if (this.table[index] === undefined) {
    this.table[index] = [];
  }
  this.table[index].push({ key, value });
};

HashTable.prototype.get = function(key) {
  const index = this.hash(key);
  if (this.table[index] !== undefined) {
    for (let pair of this.table[index]) {
      if (pair.key === key) {
        return pair.value;
      }
    }
  }
  return undefined;
};
```

Handling collisions in hash tables: part 1

```
HashTable.prototype.remove = function(key) {
  const index = this.hash(key);
  if (this.table[index] !== undefined) {
    for (let i = 0; i < this.table[index].length; i++) {
      if (this.table[index][i].key === key) {
        this.table[index].splice(i, 1);
        return true;
      }
    }
  }
  return false;
};

const ht = new HashTable();
ht.put('Alice', 25);
ht.put('Bob', 30);
ht.put('Charlie', 35);
console.log(ht.get('Bob')); // 30
ht.remove('Bob');
console.log(ht.get('Bob')); // undefined
```

Handling collisions in hash tables: Part 2

CHAPTER FOUR

When & Why to use Linked List, Tree & Graph

When Linked List?

Linked lists are commonly used in JavaScript projects for implementing data structures like stacks, queues, and hash tables. Here are some examples of how linked lists can be used in a real-world JavaScript project:

1. **Browser History:**

   A browser history can be implemented using a doubly linked list. Each node in the linked list can contain the URL, timestamp, and other relevant information about a visited web page. When the user goes back or forward, the current position in the linked list can be adjusted to display the appropriate page.
2. **Music Player:**

   A music player can use a linked list to maintain a playlist of songs. Each node in the linked list can contain information about a song, such as the artist, album, and track name. The next and previous pointers can be used to navigate between songs in the playlist.

3. **Undo/Redo Feature:**

   In an application that supports undo and redo operations, a linked list can be used to store the state of the application at different points in time. Each node in the linked list can contain a snapshot of the application state, and the next and previous pointers can be used to navigate between different states.

4. **Cache:**

   In a caching system, a linked list can be used to store frequently accessed data. When a new data item is accessed, it can be added to the head of the linked list. If the linked list exceeds a certain size, the tail of the linked list can be removed to make space for new data.

These are just a few examples of how linked lists can be used in real-world JavaScript projects. The versatility and flexibility of linked lists make them a powerful data structure for a wide range of applications.

Why Linked List?

Linked lists have several advantages over other data structures, and these advantages make them a good fit for the scenarios mentioned in my previous response:

1. **Dynamic Size:**

   Linked lists have a dynamic size, which means that they can

grow or shrink as needed. This makes them an ideal data structure for scenarios where the size of the data is not known in advance.

2. **Efficient Insertion and Deletion:**

   Linked lists can insert or delete an element in constant time, O(1), at any position in the list, which makes them more efficient than arrays for scenarios where frequent insertion or deletion is required.

3. **Efficient Memory Usage:**

   Linked lists use memory efficiently because each node only contains the data and a pointer to the next node, which saves space compared to arrays, which require a contiguous block of memory.

4. **Easy to Traverse:**

   Linked lists are easy to traverse because each node contains a pointer to the next node. This makes it easy to iterate through the entire list, search for a specific element, or navigate back and forth between nodes.

Overall, linked lists are a versatile and efficient data structure that can be used in a wide range of applications. Their dynamic size, efficient insertion and deletion, efficient memory usage, and ease of traversal make them an ideal choice for scenarios where these properties are important, such as browser history, music player, undo/redo feature, and caching systems.

When Tree?

Trees are commonly used in JavaScript projects for organizing data hierarchically. Here are some examples of how trees can be used in a real-world JavaScript project:

1. **File System:**

   A file system can be implemented using a tree data structure. Each node in the tree can represent a file or directory, with the root node representing the root directory. The parent-child relationship between nodes represents the hierarchical relationship between directories and files.
2. **HTML DOM:**

   The HTML Document Object Model (DOM) is a tree data structure that represents the structure of an HTML document. Each node in the DOM represents an HTML element, with the root node representing the HTML document itself. The parent-child relationship between nodes represents the hierarchical relationship between HTML elements.

3. **Routing in Web Applications:**

   Web applications often use a tree data structure to represent the routing hierarchy of different pages. Each node in the tree represents a page or a group of pages, with the root node representing the home page. The parent-child relationship between nodes represents the hierarchical relationship between pages.

4. **Decision Trees:**

In machine learning, decision trees are used to make decisions based on a set of rules. Each node in the tree represents a decision based on a rule, with the child nodes representing the possible outcomes of the decision.

These are just a few examples of how trees can be used in real-world JavaScript projects. The hierarchical organization and efficient searching capabilities of trees make them a powerful data structure for a wide range of applications.

Why Tree?

The advantage of using a tree data structure in the scenarios mentioned in my previous response is that it provides an efficient and hierarchical way to organize data. Here are some specific advantages of using trees:

1. **Efficient Search and Insertion:**

   Trees are designed to allow for efficient search and insertion of data. This makes them a great choice for scenarios where you need to quickly find and insert data. For example, in a file system, you can quickly search for a specific file by traversing the tree structure from the root node.

2. **Hierarchical Organization:**

   Trees allow for hierarchical organization of data. This makes them an ideal choice for scenarios where you need to organize data in a structured and logical manner. For example, in a web application, you can use a tree structure to represent the hierarchy of different pages and their relationships to each other.

3. **Scalability:**

   Trees are scalable and can handle a large amount of data efficiently. This makes them a good choice for scenarios where you need to manage large amounts of data, such as in a file system or a web application.

4. **Decision Making:**

   Trees can be used for decision making and rule-based systems. This makes them a good choice for scenarios where you need to make decisions based on a set of rules or conditions, such as in a machine learning algorithm.

Overall, trees provide an efficient and scalable way to organize and manage data in a hierarchical manner. They are a versatile data structure that can be used in a wide range of applications, from file systems and web applications to machine learning algorithms and decision-making systems.

When Graph?

Graphs are used in many real-world JavaScript projects, including:

1. **Social Networks:**

   Social networks like Facebook and LinkedIn use graph data

structures to represent the relationships between users. Each user is represented as a node, and the connections between users are represented as edges.

2. **Maps and Navigation:**

   Maps and navigation systems use graphs to represent the physical connections between different locations. Each location is represented as a node, and the physical connections between locations, such as roads or railways, are represented as edges.

3. **Data Visualization:**

   Data visualization libraries like D3.js use graphs to represent data in a visual and interactive way. Each data point is represented as a node, and the relationships between data points are represented as edges.

4. **Recommendation Systems:**

   Recommendation systems use graph data structures to represent the relationships between different items. Each item is represented as a node, and the relationships between items, such as similarities or preferences, are represented as edges.

These are just a few examples of how graphs can be used in real-world JavaScript projects. Graphs are a powerful data structure that can be used in many different applications to represent complex relationships and connections between data points.

Why Graphs?

There are several advantages to using a graph data structure in the scenarios mentioned above:

1. **Relationship Representation:**

   Graphs are well-suited for representing relationships between data points. This makes them an ideal choice for applications where data relationships are important, such as social networks and recommendation systems.

2. **Scalability:**

   Graphs are scalable and can handle a large amount of data efficiently. This makes them a good choice for applications where there is a lot of data to be processed, such as in maps and navigation systems.

3. **Visualization:**

   Graphs are easily visualized, which makes them useful for data visualization applications. By representing data points as nodes and relationships as edges, it's easy to create visualizations that help users understand complex data relationships.

4. **Efficiency:**

   Graph algorithms are often efficient and can be used to solve many types of problems, such as shortest path problems and network flow problems. This makes graphs a versatile data structure that can be used in a wide range of applications.

Overall, the advantages of using a graph data structure depend on the specific application. However, in general, graphs are a powerful tool for representing complex relationships and can be used to solve many types of problems efficiently.

CHAPTER FIVE

The Surprising Truth About Data Structures and Algorithms: Why There Are Only 50 Problems You Need to Know

Data structures and algorithms (DSA) is an essential topic for any computer science student or programmer. It is the foundation of problem-solving, programming, and software development. DSA refers to the study of organizing and manipulating data effectively in computer memory and designing algorithms for solving computational problems efficiently. It is a wide field, but if you dive into it, you'll find that there are not more than 50 DSA coding problems that you need to understand.

Learning DSA is essential because it helps in improving the efficiency of your code, reduces the time complexity of your programs, and enhances your problem-solving skills. When you start learning DSA, it might seem like a vast topic, but with time, you'll realize that it is not as complicated as it looks.

There are some essential data structures that you should be familiar with, such as arrays, linked lists, stacks, queues, trees, and graphs. Along with these data structures, you should also know the various algorithms used to manipulate these data structures, such as searching, sorting, and traversal algorithms.

As you progress in your DSA learning journey, you'll come across many coding problems. These coding problems can be broadly classified into various categories, such as arrays, strings, linked lists, trees, graphs, and dynamic programming. In each category, there are some fundamental problems that you need to solve, and once you understand the logic behind solving these problems, you'll be able to solve more complex problems.

It is essential to practice DSA problems regularly to get a better understanding of the concepts. You can practice DSA problems on various online platforms, such as HackerRank, LeetCode, CodeChef, etc. These platforms offer a vast array of problems for you to solve, and they also have discussion forums where you can interact with other programmers and learn from them.

In conclusion, DSA is an important topic for any computer science student or programmer. Though it might seem like a vast topic, there are not more than 50 DSA coding problems that you need to understand. Once you get a grip on the essential data structures and algorithms, you can solve more complex problems with ease. So, practice regularly, and you'll be on your way to becoming a proficient programmer.

CHAPTER SIX

The top 100 DSA problems that are frequently asked in a coding interview

1. **Two Sum:**

   Given an array of integers, find two numbers that add up to a specific target. Approach: Use a hash table to store the difference between the target and the current number as the key and the index as the value. Then check if the difference exists in the hash table for each number in the array.

2. **Maximum Subarray:**

   Given an array of integers, find the contiguous subarray with the largest sum. Approach: Use Kadane's algorithm to iterate through the array and keep track of the maximum subarray sum seen so far.

3. **Reverse Integer:**

Given an integer, reverse the digits of the integer. Approach: Use modulo and division to extract and reverse each digit of the integer.

4. **Palindrome Number:**

   Given an integer, determine if it is a palindrome. Approach: Convert the integer to a string and check if the string is equal to its reverse.

5. **Merge Two Sorted Lists:**

   Given two sorted linked lists, merge them into a single sorted linked list. Approach: Use a dummy node to create the new linked list and iterate through both lists, comparing the values of the current nodes and adding the smaller one to the new list.

6. **Validate Binary Search Tree:**

   Given a binary tree, determine if it is a valid binary search tree. Approach: Use recursion to check if each node satisfies the binary search tree property, where the left subtree contains only values smaller than the current node, and the right subtree contains only values larger than the current node.

7. **Climbing Stairs:**

   Given a staircase with n steps, determine the number of ways to climb to the top, where each step can be climbed with 1 or 2 steps. Approach: Use dynamic programming to store the number of ways to climb to each step, where the number of ways to reach step i is the sum of the number of ways to reach step i-1 and step i-2.

8. **Longest Common Prefix:**

   Given an array of strings, find the longest common prefix among them. Approach: Iterate through the first string and compare each character to the corresponding characters in the other strings until a mismatch is found.

9. **Remove Duplicates from Sorted Array:**

   Given a sorted array, remove the duplicates in place and return the new length of the array. Approach: Use two pointers to keep track of the current and next unique elements, and move them accordingly.

10. **Implement Queue using Stacks:**

    Implement a queue data structure using two stacks. Approach: Use one stack to push and pop elements and another stack to reverse the order of the elements when dequeueing.

11. **Intersection of Two Arrays:**

    Given two arrays, write a function to compute their intersection. Approach: Use a hash set to store the elements of the first array and check if the elements of the second array are in the hash set.

12. **Valid Parentheses:**

    Given a string containing only parentheses, determine if it is valid. Approach: Use a stack to keep track of the opening parentheses, and pop the stack when a closing parentheses is encountered.

13. **Linked List Cycle:**

Given a linked list, determine if it has a cycle in it. Approach: Use two pointers, a slow pointer and a fast pointer, to traverse the linked list. If the fast pointer catches up to the slow pointer, there is a cycle.

14. **Power of Two:**

    Given an integer, determine if it is a power of two. Approach: Use bit manipulation to check if the integer is a power of two, by checking if there is only one bit set in the binary representation of the integer.

15. **Symmetric Tree:**

    Given a binary tree, check if it is a symmetric tree. Approach: Use recursion to compare the left subtree and the right subtree of the root, by comparing their values and their left and right subtrees.

16. **Reverse Linked List:**

    Given a linked list, reverse it. Approach: Use three pointers, one for the current node, one for the previous node, and one for the next node, to traverse the linked list and reverse the pointers.

17. **Merge Sorted Array:**

    Given two sorted arrays, merge them into a single sorted array. Approach: Use two pointers to iterate through both arrays, comparing the values of the current elements and adding the smaller one to the new array.

18. **Diameter of Binary Tree:**

    Given a binary tree, determine the diameter of the tree, which is the longest path between any two nodes. Approach: Use recursion to calculate the height of each node and the diameter of each subtree, and keep track of the maximum diameter seen so far.

19. **Majority Element:**

    Given an array of integers, find the majority element, which appears more than n/2 times, where n is the length of the array. Approach: Use a hash table to count the occurrences of each element in the array, and return the element with the maximum count.

20. **Valid Anagram:**

    Given two strings, determine if they are anagrams of each other. Approach: Use a hash table to count the occurrences of each character in the first string, and subtract the occurrences of each character in the second string. If all counts are zero, the strings are anagrams.

21. **Remove Duplicates from Sorted Array:**

    Given a sorted array, remove the duplicates in-place such that each element appears only once and return the new length. Approach: Use two pointers to iterate through the array, copying non-duplicate elements to the front of the array.

22. **Best Time to Buy and Sell Stock:**

    Given an array of stock prices, find the maximum profit that can be made by buying and selling one share of the stock. Approach: Use a variable to keep track of the minimum price seen so far, and update the maximum profit seen so far as the difference between the current price and the minimum price.

23. **Climbing Stairs:**

Given n stairs, you can either climb 1 or 2 steps at a time. How many distinct ways can you climb to the top? Approach: Use dynamic programming to calculate the number of ways to climb to each step, based on the number of ways to climb to the previous two steps.

24. **Two Sum:**

Given an array of integers, find two numbers such that they add up to a specific target number. Approach: Use a hash table to store the difference between each element and the target number, and check if each subsequent element is in the hash table.

25. **Maximum Subarray:**

Given an array of integers, find the contiguous subarray with the largest sum. Approach: Use dynamic programming to calculate the maximum sum seen so far, and update it based on the current element and the maximum sum seen so far.

26. **Rotate Array:**

Given an array, rotate the array to the right by k steps, where k is non-negative. Approach: Use reverse operations on the array, first reversing the entire array, then reversing the first k elements, and finally reversing the remaining elements.

27. **Palindrome Number:**

Given an integer, determine if it is a palindrome. Approach: Convert the integer to a string and check if the string is equal to its reverse.

28. **Valid Sudoku:**

    Given a 9x9 Sudoku board, determine if it is valid. Approach: Use hash sets to check if each row, column, and 3x3 sub-box contains valid digits.

29. **Merge Two Sorted Lists:**

    Given two sorted linked lists, merge them into a single sorted linked list. Approach: Use two pointers to iterate through both linked lists, comparing the values of the current nodes and adding the smaller one to the new linked list.

30. **Pascal's Triangle:**

    Given a non-negative integer numRows, generate the first numRows of Pascal's triangle. Approach: Use dynamic programming to calculate each row of Pascal's triangle based on the previous row.

31. **Valid Perfect Square:**

    Given a positive integer num, determine if it is a perfect square. Approach: Use binary search to check if the square of each middle element is equal to the target number.

32. **Reverse Integer:**

    Given a 32-bit signed integer, reverse the digits of the integer. Approach: Use modulo and division to extract the digits of the integer in reverse order and construct the reversed integer.

33. **Implement Queue using Stacks:**

    Implement a first-in-first-out (FIFO) queue using only two stacks. Approach: Use two stacks to maintain the order of elements, pushing elements onto one stack and popping elements from the other stack.

34. **Longest Common Prefix:**

    Given an array of strings, find the longest common prefix among them. Approach: Compare the characters of each string in the array from left to right, stopping at the first non-matching character.

35. **Count and Say:**

    Given an integer n, generate the nth term of the count-and-say sequence. Approach: Use recursion to generate each term of the sequence based on the previous term.

36. **Symmetric Tree:**

    Given a binary tree, check whether it is a mirror of itself (ie, symmetric around its center). Approach: Use recursion to compare the left and right subtrees, checking if their values are equal and if their children are mirrored.

37. **Intersection of Two Linked Lists:**

    Given two linked lists, find their intersection node. Approach: Use two pointers to iterate through both linked lists, starting at the head of each list and resetting to the head of the other list once they reach the end.

38. **Same Tree:**

Given two binary trees, write a function to check if they are the same or not. Approach: Use recursion to compare each node of the two trees, checking if their values are equal and if their children are the same.

39. **Climbing Stairs (Optimized):**

Given n stairs, you can either climb 1 or 2 steps at a time. How many distinct ways can you climb to the top? Approach: Use dynamic programming to calculate the number of ways to climb to each step, based on the number of ways to climb to the previous step.

40. **Implement Stack using Queues:**

Implement a last-in-first-out (LIFO) stack using only two queues. Approach: Use two queues to maintain the order of elements, pushing elements onto one queue and popping elements from the other queue.

41. **Maximum Depth of Binary Tree:**

Given a binary tree, find its maximum depth. Approach: Use recursion to calculate the maximum depth of the left and right subtrees, adding 1 to the larger depth.

42. **Valid Parentheses:**

Given a string containing just the characters '(', ')', '{', '}', '[' and ']', determine if the input string is valid. Approach: Use a stack to keep track of the opening parentheses and check if each closing parenthesis matches the last opening parenthesis.

43. **Min Stack:**

    Design a stack that supports push, pop, top, and retrieving the minimum element in constant time. Approach: Use two stacks to maintain the elements and their minimum values.

44. **Reverse Linked List:**

    Reverse a singly linked list. Approach: Use three pointers to iterate through the linked list, reversing the direction of the pointers at each step.

45. **Add Two Numbers:**

    Given two non-empty linked lists representing two non-negative integers, add the two numbers and return the sum as a linked list. Approach: Use two pointers to iterate through both linked lists, adding the values of each node and carrying over the remainder to the next node.

46. **Maximum Product Subarray:**

    Given an integer array nums, find the contiguous subarray within an array (containing at least one number) which has the largest product. Approach: Use dynamic programming to calculate the maximum and minimum products seen so far, and update them based on the current element and the maximum and minimum products seen so far.

47. **Reverse Words in a String:**

    Given an input string, reverse the string word by word. Approach: Split the string into individual words, reverse the order of the words, and join them back together.

48. **Linked List Cycle:**

    Given a linked list, determine if it has a cycle in it. Approach: Use two pointers, one moving at twice the speed of the other, to detect if the two pointers meet at the same node.

49. **Remove Nth Node From End of List:**

    Given a linked list, remove the n-th node from the end of list and return its head. Approach: Use two pointers, one moving n steps ahead of the other, to reach the n-th node from the end and remove it.

50. **Valid Anagram:**

    Given two strings s and t, write a function to determine if t is an anagram

51. **Single Number:**

    Given a non-empty array of integers, every element appears twice except for one. Find that single one. Approach: Use XOR to cancel out the duplicate elements and find the single element.

52. **Binary Tree Maximum Path Sum:**

    Given a non-empty binary tree, find the maximum path sum. Approach: Use recursion to calculate the maximum path sum for each node, and update the maximum path sum seen so far based on the sum of the left and right subtrees.

53. **Maximum Subarray:**

    Given an integer array nums, find the contiguous subarray (containing at least one number) which has the largest sum and return its sum. Approach: Use dynamic programming to calculate the maximum subarray sum seen so far, and update it based on the current element and the maximum subarray sum seen so far.

54. **Merge Two Sorted Lists:**

    Merge two sorted linked lists and return it as a new sorted list. Approach: Use two pointers to iterate through both linked lists, adding the smaller node to a new linked list and moving the corresponding pointer forward.

55. **Longest Common Prefix:**

    Write a function to find the longest common prefix string amongst an array of strings. Approach: Iterate through the first string, comparing each character with the corresponding character of the other strings, and returning the prefix when a mismatch is found.

56. **Group Anagrams:**

    Given an array of strings, group anagrams together. Approach: Use a hashmap to group the anagrams by their sorted forms.

57. **Reverse Integer:**

    Given a 32-bit signed integer, reverse digits of an integer. Approach: Use mod and division to extract each digit and reverse the order of the digits.

58. **Power of Two:**

    Given an integer, write a function to determine if it is a power of two. Approach: Use bit manipulation to check if the integer has only one bit set.

59. **Palindrome Linked List:**

    Given a singly linked list, determine if it is a palindrome. Approach: Use a stack to store the first half of the linked list, and compare it with the second half.

60. **Two Sum:**

    Given an array of integers, return indices of the two numbers such that they add up to a specific target. Approach: Use a hashmap to store the complement of each number and check if the complement exists in the hashmap.

61. **Intersection of Two Arrays:**

    Given two arrays, write a function to compute their intersection. Approach: Use a set to store the elements of the first array, and check if each element of the second array exists in the set.

62. **Lowest Common Ancestor of a Binary Tree:**

    Given a binary tree, find the lowest common ancestor (LCA) of two given nodes in the tree. Approach: Use recursion to find the LCA in the left and right subtrees, returning the node itself or null if the node is not found.

63. **Merge Intervals:**

    Given a collection of intervals, merge overlapping intervals. Approach: Sort the intervals by their start times, and merge overlapping intervals by updating their end times.

64. **Valid Sudoku:**

    Determine if a 9x9 Sudoku board is valid. Approach: Check if each row, column, and 3x3 sub-box contains only the digits 1-9, without duplicates.

65. **Count and Say:**

    The count-and-say sequence is the sequence of integers with the first five terms as following: 1, 11, 21, 1211, 111221. Approach: Use recursion to generate the next term of the sequence based on the previous term.

66. **First Missing Positive:**

    Given an unsorted integer array nums, find the smallest missing positive integer. Approach: Use bucket sort to

67. **Validate Binary Search Tree:**

    Given a binary tree, determine if it is a valid binary search tree (BST). Approach: Use recursion to check if each node satisfies the BST property, which states that the left subtree contains only values less than the node, and the right subtree contains only values greater than the node.

68. **Permutations:**

    Given an array nums of distinct integers, return all the possible permutations. Approach: Use recursion to generate all possible permutations by swapping elements.

69. **Climbing Stairs:**

    You are climbing a staircase. It takes n steps to reach the top.

Each time you can either climb 1 or 2 steps. In how many distinct ways can you climb to the top? Approach: Use dynamic programming to calculate the number of distinct ways to climb to the ith step based on the number of distinct ways to climb to the (i-1)th and (i-2)th steps.

70. **Search in Rotated Sorted Array:**

Suppose an array of length n sorted in ascending order is rotated between 1 and n times. Given a target value, return the index if it is found in the array, otherwise return -1. Approach: Use binary search to find the pivot point where the array is rotated, and then search for the target in the appropriate half of the array.

71. **Majority Element:**

Given an array of size n, find the majority element. The majority element is the element that appears more than n/2 times. Approach: Use Boyer-Moore Voting Algorithm to find the majority element in a single pass.

72. **Symmetric Tree:**

Given a binary tree, check whether it is a mirror of itself (ie, symmetric around its center). Approach: Use recursion to check if the left subtree is a mirror of the right subtree, and vice versa.

73. **Valid Parentheses:**

Given a string containing just the characters '(', ')', '{', '}', '[' and ']', determine if the input string is valid. Approach: Use a stack to keep track of opening parentheses and pop them when a closing parenthesis is encountered.

74. **Word Search:**

    Given an m x n grid of characters board and a string word, return true if word exists in the grid. Approach: Use DFS to search for the word in the grid, backtracking when a dead end is encountered.

75. **Product of Array Except Self:**

    Given an integer array nums, return an array output such that output[i] is equal to the product of all the elements of nums except nums[i]. Approach: Use two passes to calculate the product of all elements to the left and right of each element, and multiply them together to get the final product.

76. **Container With Most Water:**

    Given n non-negative integers a1, a2, ..., an , where each represents a point at coordinate (i, ai). n vertical lines are drawn such that the two endpoints of the line i is at (i, ai) and (i, 0). Find two lines, which, together with the x-axis forms a container, such that the container contains the most water. Approach: Use two pointers to keep track of the left and right indices, and update the maximum area seen so far based on the area of the current container.

77. **Merge k Sorted Lists:**

    Given an array of k linked lists, merge them into a single linked list that is sorted in ascending order. Approach: Use a priority queue to store the smallest element from each linked list, and continue to pop elements and add them to the result list until all lists are exhausted.

78. **Word Break:**

Given a non-empty string s and a dictionary wordDict containing a list of non-empty words, determine if s can be segmented into a space-separated sequence of one or more dictionary words. Approach: Use dynamic programming to check if a substring can be segmented into valid words by checking if the prefix is in the dictionary and the suffix can be segmented.

79. **Counting Elements:**

Given an integer array arr, count element x such that x + 1 is also in arr. Approach: Use a hash set to store all elements in arr, and iterate through arr to check if each element + 1 is in the set.

80. **Maximum Subarray:**

Given an integer array nums, find the contiguous subarray (containing at least one number) which has the largest sum and return its sum. Approach: Use Kadane's Algorithm to find the maximum sum subarray in a single pass.

81. **Kth Largest Element in an Array:**

Find the kth largest element in an unsorted array. Note that it is the kth largest element in the sorted order, not the kth distinct element. Approach: Use quickselect algorithm to partition the array into smaller and larger elements relative to a pivot, until the pivot index is equal to k.

82. **Min Stack:**

Design a stack that supports push, pop, top, and retrieving the minimum element in constant time. Approach: Use two stacks to keep track of the elements and the minimum element seen so far.

83. **Maximum Depth of Binary Tree:**

    Given the root of a binary tree, return its maximum depth. Approach: Use recursion to calculate the maximum depth of the left and right subtrees, and return the maximum of the two plus one for the current node.

84. **Sort Colors:**

    Given an array nums with n objects colored red, white, or blue, sort them in-place so that objects of the same color are adjacent, with the colors in the order red, white, and blue. Approach: Use three pointers to keep track of the boundaries between red, white, and blue elements, and swap elements accordingly.

85. **First Missing Positive:**

    Given an unsorted integer array nums, find the smallest missing positive integer. Approach: Use a hash set to store all positive elements in nums, and iterate through positive integers starting from 1 until the first missing integer is found.

86. **Letter Combinations of a Phone Number:**

    Given a string containing digits from 2-9 inclusive, return all possible letter combinations that the number could represent. Approach: Use recursion to generate all possible combinations by appending each possible letter to the current string. Use a mapping of digits to letters to generate the possible letters for each digit.

87. **Unique Paths:**

A robot is located at the top-left corner of a m x n grid. The robot can only move either down or right at any point in time. The robot is trying to reach the bottom-right corner of the grid. How many possible unique paths are there? Approach: Use dynamic programming to calculate the number of unique paths to each cell by summing the number of unique paths from the cell above and to the left.

88. **House Robber:**

You are a professional robber planning to rob houses along a street. Each house has a certain amount of money stashed. All houses at this place are arranged in a circle. That means the first house is the neighbor of the last one. Meanwhile, adjacent houses have a security system connected, and it will automatically contact the police if two adjacent houses were broken into on the same night. Given a list of non-negative integers nums representing the amount of money of each house, return the maximum amount of money you can rob tonight without alerting the police. Approach: Use dynamic programming to calculate the maximum amount of money that can be robbed from the houses up to a given index, taking into account the fact that the first and last houses are adjacent.

89. **Merge Intervals:**

Given an array of intervals where intervals[i] = [starti, endi], merge all overlapping intervals, and return an array of the non-overlapping intervals that cover all the intervals in the input. Approach: Sort the intervals by their start times, and iterate through the sorted intervals to merge overlapping intervals.

90. **Pow(x, n):**

Implement pow(x, n), which calculates x raised to the power n (i.e., xn). Approach: Use binary exponentiation to calculate the result recursively, by squaring the result at each step and reducing the exponent by half.

91. **Reorder List:**

Given a singly linked list L: L0→L1→...→Ln-1→Ln, reorder it to: L0→Ln→L1→Ln-1→L2→Ln-2→... Approach: Use two pointers to find the middle of the linked list, reverse the second half of the list, and then merge the first and second halves of the list by alternating nodes.

92. **Rotate Array:**

Given an array, rotate the array to the right by k steps, where k is non-negative. Approach: Reverse the entire array, then reverse the first k elements and the last n-k elements separately.

93. **Intersection of Two Linked Lists:**

Write a program to find the node at which the intersection of two singly linked lists begins. Approach: Traverse both linked lists to find their lengths and their tail nodes, and then adjust the starting point of the longer linked list so that both lists have the same length. Then, traverse both linked lists in tandem until the intersection node is found.

94. **Flatten Binary Tree to Linked List:**

Given the root of a binary tree, flatten the tree into a "linked list": the left child of each node is null, and the right child is the next node in preorder traversal. Approach: Use recursion to flatten the left and right subtrees, and then rewire the left and right subtrees to form the flattened linked list.

95. **Subsets:**

Given an integer array nums of unique elements, return all possible subsets (the power set). Approach: Use backtracking to generate all possible subsets by including or excluding each element in the array.

96. **Best Time to Buy and Sell Stock:**

You are given an array prices where prices[i] is the price of a given stock on the ith day. You want to maximize your profit by choosing a single day to buy one stock and choosing a

97. **Counting Elements:**

Given an integer array arr, count element x such that x + 1 is also in arr. If there're duplicates in arr, count them separately. Approach: Use a hash set to store all elements in the array, and then iterate through the array to count the number of elements that have a corresponding x+1 element in the set.

98. **Maximum Subarray:**

Given an integer array nums, find the contiguous subarray (containing at least one number) which has the largest sum and return its sum. Approach: Use dynamic programming to calculate the maximum subarray sum up to each index, and keep track of the maximum subarray sum seen so far.

99. **Climbing Stairs:**

You are climbing a staircase. It takes n steps to reach the top.

Each time you can either climb 1 or 2 steps. In how many distinct ways can you climb to the top? Approach: Use dynamic programming to calculate the number of distinct ways to climb to each step, by summing the number of distinct ways from the previous two steps.

100. **Valid Parentheses:**

Given a string s containing just the characters '(', ')', '{', '}', '[' and ']', determine if the input string is valid. An input string is valid if: Open brackets must be closed by the same type of brackets. Open brackets must be closed in the correct order. Approach: Use a stack to keep track of the opening brackets encountered, and match them with the closing brackets encountered. If a closing bracket does not match the top of the stack, the string is not valid.

CHAPTER SEVEN

DBMS (Database Management System)

Introduction:

Database Management System (DBMS) is a software application used for managing and organizing data. A database is a collection of data that is stored in a structured way, which makes it easier to access, manage and update. DBMS is an essential component of many applications, ranging from small personal applications to large enterprise applications.

In this chapter, we will discuss why it is important to prepare for DBMS and how to prepare for it. We will cover the basics of databases, designing a database, optimizing a database, and the different types of DBMS. We will also discuss the importance of knowing SQL or no SQL and their differences.

Basics of Databases:

Before you start preparing for DBMS, it is important to understand the basics of databases. Databases are used to store data in a structured way so that it can be easily accessed, managed and updated. You should understand the different operations of the database, such as adding, deleting, modifying, and retrieving data. It is also important to understand how to link data between more than one tables or collections.

Designing a Database:

Designing a database is an important aspect of DBMS. A well-designed database ensures that data is stored in a structured way that makes it easy to access, manage and update. Normalization is the process of designing a database to reduce redundancy and dependency. There are different normal forms, including 1NF, 2NF, 3NF and BCNF, which are used to optimize the design of a database. It is important to understand these normal forms and how to apply them to your database design.

Optimizing a Database:

Optimizing a database is the process of improving its performance. This can be done by using indexes, replica sets, sharding, and other techniques. Indexes are used to speed up data retrieval by creating a data structure that allows for quick access to data. Replica sets are used to increase availability and provide redundancy, while sharding is used to partition data across multiple servers.

Knowing SQL or No SQL:

SQL and No SQL are two types of DBMS that are widely used. SQL stands for Structured Query Language and is used for relational databases, such as MySQL or MsSQL. No SQL, on the other hand, stands for Not Only SQL and is used for non-relational databases, such as MongoDB or CouchDB. It is important to have a basic understanding of both SQL and No SQL, as they are used in different applications and scenarios.

Preparing for DBMS:

To prepare for DBMS, it is important to have a good understanding of the basics of databases, database design, and optimization techniques. You should also have a basic understanding of SQL or No SQL, depending on the type of database you are working with. There are several ways to prepare for DBMS, including taking online courses, attending workshops, reading books and articles, and practicing with hands-on projects.

Conclusion:

DBMS is an essential component of many applications, ranging from small personal applications to large enterprise applications. To prepare for DBMS, you should have a good understanding of the basics of databases, database design, optimization techniques, and SQL or No SQL. There are several ways to prepare for DBMS, including taking online courses, attending workshops, reading books and articles, and practicing with hands-on projects. By preparing for DBMS, you will be well-equipped to design, manage, and optimize databases for different applications and scenarios.

10 Basic questions of DBMS:

1. What is a database?
2. Why are databases used?
3. What kind of data can be stored in a database?
4. What are the different types of operations that can be performed on a database?
5. What is normalization and why is it important?
6. What are the different levels of normalization?
7. What is a primary key in a database?
8. What is a foreign key in a database?
9. What is a join in a database and how does it work?

10. What is indexing in a database and why is it important?

10 Normalization questions:

1. What is normalization in a database?
2. Why is normalization important in database design?
3. What are the different normal forms and how do they differ from each other?
4. What is First Normal Form (1NF)?
5. What is Second Normal Form (2NF)?
6. What is Third Normal Form (3NF)?
7. What is Boyce-Codd Normal Form (BCNF)?
8. What is a functional dependency in a database and how does it relate to normalization?
9. What is denormalization and when is it appropriate to use it?
10. What are some common pitfalls to avoid when normalizing a database?

10 Database Design Questions:

1. What is database design?
2. What are the different types of database design?
3. What is the purpose of a database schema?
4. What are the different components of a database schema?
5. What are the different types of relationships between tables in a database?
6. What is an Entity-Relationship (ER) diagram and how is it used in database design?

7. What is a database model and how does it help in designing a database?
8. What are the different types of database models?
9. What is database normalization and how does it impact database design?
10. What are some common design considerations for databases, such as data types, indexing, and constraints?

SQL:

1. What is SQL and how is it used in database management?
2. What is a relational database and how does it differ from other types of databases?
3. What are some common SQL commands used for database manipulation?
4. What is a join in SQL and how is it used to link data between tables?
5. What are some best practices for optimizing SQL queries?
6. What is a transaction in SQL and how is it used to ensure data consistency?
7. What are some common security considerations when working with SQL databases?
8. What is an index in SQL and how does it impact database performance?
9. How do you handle database backup and recovery in SQL?
10. What is the difference between SQL and NoSQL databases?

NoSQL:

1. What is NoSQL and how is it used in database management?

2. What are the different types of NoSQL databases and how do they differ from each other?
3. What are some common NoSQL data models?
4. What are some best practices for optimizing NoSQL queries?
5. How does data consistency work in NoSQL databases?
6. What are some common security considerations when working with NoSQL databases?
7. What is sharding in NoSQL and how is it used to scale databases?
8. How do you handle database backup and recovery in NoSQL?
9. What is the difference between NoSQL and SQL databases?
10. When is it appropriate to use a NoSQL database instead of a SQL database?

Database Optimization:

1. What is database optimization and why is it important?
2. What are some common techniques used for database optimization?
3. How do you optimize database indexing for improved performance?
4. What are some best practices for designing a database schema for optimal performance?
5. What is caching and how is it used to optimize database performance?
6. How does database partitioning work and how is it used to scale databases?
7. What are some common performance bottlenecks in databases and how can they be addressed?
8. How do you monitor and tune database performance?
9. What are some common security considerations when optimizing databases?

10. How do you handle database backup and recovery in optimized databases?

Question over a real example by using SQL:

1. Suppose you are working for a company that sells products online. The company has a database that stores information about customers, orders, and products. The database consists of the following tables:

   Customers: contains information about each customer, including name, email, and address.

   Orders: contains information about each order, including the customer who placed the order, the date and time of the order, and the total price of the order.

   Order Items: contains information about each item that was ordered, including the product ID, the quantity ordered, and the price per item.

   Products: contains information about each product that the company sells, including the product name, description, and price.

   Now, suppose the company wants to generate a report that shows the total revenue generated by each product in the last quarter. Write an SQL query that would accomplish this task.

2. Suppose you are working for a hospital and the hospital wants to keep track of patient data. The hospital has a database that stores information about patients, doctors, and medical procedures.

The database consists of the following tables:

Patients: contains information about each patient, including name, age, and address.
Doctors: contains information about each doctor, including name, specialty, and contact information.
Medical Procedures: contains information about each medical procedure, including the type of procedure, the date and time it was performed, and the cost.
Appointments: contains information about each appointment, including the patient who has the appointment, the doctor who will see the patient, the date and time of the appointment, and the reason for the appointment.

Now, suppose the hospital wants to generate a report that shows the total number of appointments each doctor had in the last month, grouped by their specialty. Write an SQL query that would accomplish this task.

3. Suppose you are working for a retail company that wants to keep track of inventory levels for each of its stores. The company has a database that stores information about products, stores, and inventory levels. The database consists of the following tables:

   Products: contains information about each product, including the product name, description, and price.
   Stores: contains information about each store, including the store name, location, and contact information.
   Inventory: contains information about each product's inventory level at each store, including the product ID, the store ID, and the quantity on hand.

   Now, suppose the company wants to generate a report that shows the top-selling products for each store in the last month. Write an SQL query that would accomplish this task.

4. Suppose you are working for an e-commerce company that wants to keep track of customer data. The company has a database that stores information about customers, orders, and products. The database consists of the following tables:

   Customers: contains information about each customer, including name, email, and address.
   Orders: contains information about each order, including the order date, the customer who placed the order, and the total cost of the order.
   Products: contains information about each product, including the product name, description, and price.
   Order Details: contains information about the products included in each order, including the order ID, the product ID, and the quantity ordered.

   Now, suppose the company wants to generate a report that shows the total revenue earned from each customer in the last month. Write an SQL query that would accomplish this task.

5. Suppose you are working for a healthcare company that wants to keep track of patient information. The company has a database that stores information about patients, doctors, appointments, and medical history. The database consists of the following tables:

   Patients: contains information about each patient, including name, birthdate, and contact information.
   Doctors: contains information about each doctor, including name, specialty, and contact information.
   Appointments: contains information about each appointment, including the appointment date and time, the patient who made the appointment, and the doctor who will be seeing the patient.
   Medical History: contains information about each patient's

medical history, including the patient ID, the diagnosis, and the treatment received.

Now, suppose the company wants to generate a report that shows the number of patients each doctor has seen in the last month. Write an SQL query that would accomplish this task.

Question Using No SQL:

1. Suppose you are working for an e-commerce company that wants to store product information in a NoSQL database. The company has a database that stores information about products, including name, description, price, and categories. The database consists of the following collections:

   Products: contains information about each product, including name, description, price, and a list of categories that the product belongs to.

   Now, suppose the company wants to generate a report that shows the total sales for each category of products over the last month. Write a query that would accomplish this task using the MongoDB aggregation framework.

2. Suppose you are working for a social media platform that wants to store user profiles in a NoSQL database. The company has a database that stores information about users, including their name, email, password, interests, and followers. The database consists of the following collections:

   Users: contains information about each user, including their name, email, password, interests, and a list of their followers.

Now, suppose the company wants to identify users who share common interests, and suggest them to follow each other. Write a query that would accomplish this task using the MongoDB aggregation framework.

3. Suppose you are working for an e-commerce company that sells products online. The company wants to store customer orders in a NoSQL database. Each order contains information such as the customer's name, email, shipping address, billing address, and the items they ordered. The company wants to be able to quickly retrieve all orders for a specific customer.

   Design a NoSQL schema that would meet these requirements and explain why you chose that schema.

4. Suppose you are working for a social media platform that allows users to post updates, share photos, and follow other users. The platform needs to be able to quickly retrieve all posts by a specific user, as well as all posts that were made within a specific time frame.

   Design a NoSQL schema that would meet these requirements and explain why you chose that schema.

5. Suppose you are working for an e-commerce company that sells products online. The company needs to be able to quickly retrieve all orders for a specific customer, as well as all orders that contain a specific product.

   Design a NoSQL schema that would meet these requirements and explain why you chose that schema.

CHAPTER EIGHT

Mastering Full Stack Development with MERN/MEAN From Building Simple Demos to Solving Real Problems

Learning a full stack is one of the most sought-after skills in the tech industry today. It involves mastering a combination of different technologies and programming languages that are used to build both front-end and back-end applications. Among the full stack frameworks available, MERN and MEAN are two of the most popular. They are both highly flexible, scalable and powerful, and offer developers a wide range of options to create robust and dynamic applications. In this article, we will explore the benefits of learning a full stack, and how to go about doing it using MERN/MEAN.

The first step to learning a full stack is to choose a stack that best fits your needs. MERN stack is composed of MongoDB, Express, React, and Node.js while MEAN stack comprises of MongoDB, Express, Angular, and Node.js. Each stack has its own set of strengths and weaknesses, and it's important to choose one that aligns with your career goals and interests. Once you have chosen a stack, the next step is to start learning.

One of the most effective ways to learn a full stack is to build a simple demo application using an online course. This will give you a solid foundation of knowledge and experience with the stack. The course will take you through the basics of each component of the stack, and provide you with hands-on experience working with them. After completing the course, it's important to enhance your project with your own ideas and innovations. This will help you to better understand how the stack works, and how to optimize it for real-world use.

Once you have gained confidence with the stack, the next step is to create an application that solves a real-world problem. Finding a problem yourself and creating a solution for it is important as it will give you the confidence to talk about the problem, and it will also help you to have a great memory of your learning experience. This is because, for this project, you have thought of every bit and peace, from the problem itself to the implementation of the solution.

To create an application, start by identifying a problem that you want to solve. It could be anything, from streamlining a business process to developing a social media platform. Once you have identified the problem, break it down into smaller, manageable parts. This will help you to better understand the problem, and to develop a more targeted solution. Next, start developing your application using the skills and knowledge you have gained from the course.

While creating your application, it's important to keep a few things in mind.

Firstly, always test your code thoroughly to ensure that it works as expected. This will help you to identify and fix bugs early on in the development process. Secondly, write clean and efficient code that is easy to understand and maintain. This will make it easier for you or other developers to work on the code in the future. Finally, always be open to feedback and constructive criticism. This will help you to improve your coding skills and develop better applications.

In conclusion, learning a full stack is a highly valuable skill that can lead to a rewarding career in the tech industry. MERN and MEAN stack are two of the most popular full stack frameworks available today, offering developers a wide range of options to create robust and dynamic applications. To learn a full stack, start by choosing a stack that aligns with your career goals and interests. Then, build a simple demo application using an online course, enhance it with your own ideas and innovations, and finally, create an application that solves a real-world problem. With dedication, practice, and an open mind, anyone can master a full stack and become a highly sought-after developer.

Level Up Your Coding Game with These 10 MERN Stack Projects for Beginners:

1. **Todo App:**

   Build a simple todo application using MERN stack that allows users to add and delete tasks, and mark tasks as complete.
2. **E-commerce Website:**

   Build an e-commerce website using the MERN stack with features like product listings, shopping cart, and checkout.
3. **Blogging Platform:**

   Build a platform where users can create and publish their own blog posts, with features like comments, likes, and sharing.

4. **Social Media App:**

   Build a social media app using the MERN stack that allows users to create profiles, post updates, follow other users, and interact with each other.

5. **Recipe Sharing Platform:**

   Build a platform where users can share and discover new recipes, with features like search, filtering, and rating.

6. **Job Board:**

   Build a job board using the MERN stack that allows employers to post job openings and job seekers to apply for jobs.

7. **Real Estate Listings:**

   Build a website that displays real estate listings with features like search, filtering, and maps.

8. **Music Player:**

   Build a music player using the MERN stack that allows users to upload and play their own music files.

9. **Chat App:**

   Build a chat application using the MERN stack that allows users to send and receive messages in real-time.

10. **Weather App:**

    Build a weather app using the MERN stack that shows current weather conditions and forecasts for different locations.

These projects will help beginners to gain hands-on experience with MERN stack development and provide a solid foundation for more complex projects in the future.

CHAPTER NINE

From Rookie to Rockstar: 10 Key Strategies to Crush Your Coding Interview

Preparing for a coding interview can be a daunting task, especially for freshers who are new to the industry. However, with the right preparation strategies and techniques, you can increase your chances of success and land your dream job.

Here are 10 key points to focus on while preparing for a coding interview as a fresher:

1. **Understand the basics:** Before you start preparing for a coding interview, make sure you have a solid understanding of the basics of computer science. This includes data structures, algorithms, programming languages, and software development principles. Make sure you are comfortable with these concepts before moving on to more advanced topics.
2. **Choose your programming language:** When preparing for a coding interview, it's important to choose a programming language that you are comfortable with. This could be Java, Python, C++, or any other popular language. Make sure you have a deep understanding of the syntax and features of your chosen

language.

3. **Solve practice problems**: The best way to prepare for a coding interview is by solving practice problems. There are many resources available online, such as LeetCode, HackerRank, and CodeSignal, that provide a wide range of coding challenges to help you practice. Start with easy problems and gradually move on to more difficult ones as you gain more confidence.
4. **Focus on data structures and algorithms:** Data structures and algorithms are the foundation of computer science and are critical to success in a coding interview. Make sure you have a deep understanding of common data structures like arrays, linked lists, stacks, and queues, as well as algorithms like sorting, searching, and graph traversal.
5. **Learn to analyze problems**: In a coding interview, you will be presented with a problem that you need to solve using code. It's important to take the time to understand the problem and analyze it before you start coding. Break the problem down into smaller pieces and identify any patterns or algorithms that could be used to solve it.
6. **Write clean and efficient code:** Writing clean and efficient code is important in a coding interview. Make sure your code is easy to read and understand, uses proper variable names, and is well-structured. Also, pay attention to efficiency and try to optimize your code for speed and memory usage.
7. **Practice whiteboard coding:** In many coding interviews, you will be asked to write code on a whiteboard. This can be intimidating for some people, but it's important to practice whiteboard coding so you can get comfortable with it. Try solving practice problems on a whiteboard or practicing with a friend.
8. **Brush up on system design:** In addition to coding, many interviews will also include questions about system design. This involves designing and implementing a system architecture that meets specific requirements. Make sure you understand the basics of system design and are familiar with common

architectures like REST and microservices.

9. **Research the company and position:** Before your interview, take the time to research the company and position you are applying for. This will help you understand the company culture, values, and mission, and allow you to tailor your interview answers to the specific job requirements.
10. **Stay calm and confident:** Finally, it's important to stay calm and confident during your interview. Remember, the interviewer is not trying to trick you or make you feel bad. They are simply trying to assess your skills and abilities. Take a deep breath, stay positive, and do your best.

In conclusion, preparing for a coding interview as a fresher can be challenging, but with the right preparation strategies and techniques, you can increase your chances of success. Focus on the basics, solve practice problems, and learn to analyze problems. Also, practice writing clean and efficient code, and practice whiteboard coding. Brush up on system design and research the company and position you are applying for. Finally, stay calm and confident.

CHAPTER TEN

Part 1: Summary

3 key thing to prepare

2nd P : Publish (Building Awesome Resume & Reaching Companies)

Your resume is your first impression, and reaching out to people is your opportunity to make lasting connections. With the right mindset and a willingness to put in the effort, you can build a network of support and propel yourself towards success.

CHAPTER ELEVEN

The Call

It was a regular evening for me at the library, with my head buried in a book on algorithms. Suddenly, my phone rang, and the sound of it caught everyone's attention in the room. It turned out to be my old friend Jatin, who had called me at an ungodly hour of the night. I could sense something was wrong when I heard his voice choking with emotion.

As I probed him for what had happened, he broke down and poured his heart out to me. He revealed how his family had taken out a loan to pay for his education, and their finances had been stretched thin. Worse still, despite his best efforts, he had been unable to land a job despite having prepared for every possible technical interview question. He had put his resume on every possible online portal, but only a few adventurists had called him for job offers, asking for money instead of providing one.

I was taken aback and had no answer for his question about why companies were not calling him. I had never faced this issue myself, as I had studied at IIT, where companies came to campus for recruitment. All we had to do was to prepare for the interviews, and the rest was taken care of by the college.

I could see that Jatin was distressed, and I didn't want to leave him hanging. So, I told him that we would work on a solution and that we would discuss it first thing in the morning. I asked him to get some rest, and we would chat again with a clear mind.

That night, I spent hours researching solutions for Jatin's problem on the internet. Unfortunately, there was no direct solution to his situation, and the advice I found was vague and unhelpful. But I gathered as much information as I could, and I decided to contact some of my seniors who could offer better guidance.

When Jatin called me the next morning, I had only slept for a few hours. However, it was an urgent call, and I picked up, hoping to share some good news with him. He was anxious to know if I had figured out a way to solve his problem. I asked him if he had gotten enough sleep, and he replied that he had managed to get a little.

Then he reminded me of my promise to help him find a solution. I began to share the information I had gathered the previous night.

CHAPTER TWELVE

Crafting a Masterpiece: How to Create a Signature Resume That Gets You Noticed

A resume is an essential document that showcases your education, work experience, and skills to potential employers. It is your first impression on the recruiters and HR managers. Therefore, it is crucial to create a resume that stands out from the crowd and portrays your unique strengths and capabilities. Creating a signature resume is the key to catch the attention of potential employers and get hired for your dream job. In this article, we will discuss some tips and tricks to create a signature resume that will help you stand out from the rest.

1. Tailor your resume to the job

The first step to creating a signature resume is to tailor it to the job you are applying for. You should research the company and the position you are interested in and modify your resume to match the job requirements. This will demonstrate to the recruiter that you are a good fit for the position and that you have the relevant skills and experience needed for the job.

2. Highlight your achievements

Instead of just listing your job responsibilities, focus on your accomplishments and how you have added value to your previous employers. This could be in the form of increased sales, improved processes, or any other achievements that demonstrate your skills and abilities. This will make your resume stand out and give the recruiter a better idea of what you can bring to the table.

3. Use keywords

Many companies use applicant tracking systems (ATS) to screen resumes before they even reach the hiring manager. These systems look for specific keywords that match the job description. Therefore, it is essential to include keywords in your resume that are relevant to the job. This will increase your chances of getting past the ATS and landing an interview.

4. Use a professional format

The format of your resume is crucial as it is the first thing the recruiter will see. It should be professional, easy to read, and visually appealing. Use a clear font and make sure the layout is consistent throughout the document. You can also use bold, italics, and bullet points to highlight important information and make it easier for the recruiter to scan.

5. Add a personal touch

Adding a personal touch to your resume can make it stand out and give the recruiter an insight into your personality. This could be in the form of a personal statement, a hobbies section, or any other information that sets you apart from other candidates. However, make sure it is relevant to the job and does not distract from your qualifications.

4. Include relevant certifications and courses

Adding relevant certifications and courses to your resume can demonstrate your commitment to learning and your expertise in a particular area. This can make you stand out from other candidates and give the recruiter a better idea of your skills and abilities.

5. Proofread and edit

Finally, it is essential to proofread and edit your resume before sending it out. Typos and grammatical errors can make you appear unprofessional and careless. Take the time to review your resume and ensure it is error-free and polished.

In conclusion, creating a signature resume is essential in today's job market, where the competition is fierce. By tailoring your resume to the job, highlighting your achievements, using keywords, using a professional format, adding a personal touch, including relevant certifications and courses, and proofreading and editing, you can create a resume that stands out from the crowd and gets you noticed by potential employers. Remember to showcase your unique strengths and capabilities, and demonstrate how you can add value to the company. With a signature resume, you can take the first step towards landing your dream job.

CHAPTER THIRTEEN

Less is More: Why Obvious Information Doesn't Belong in Your Resume

In today's highly competitive job market, creating a strong and impressive resume is crucial to getting noticed by potential employers. However, many job seekers make the mistake of including obvious information in their resumes that can actually detract from their overall message. It's important to understand that a resume is not a comprehensive biography, but rather a concise and focused document that highlights your most important skills and accomplishments. In this article, we'll explore why you should avoid including obvious information in your resume, and provide tips for creating a more effective and impactful document.

One of the most common mistakes job seekers make is including too much information in their resumes. This can make it difficult for hiring managers to quickly identify your most relevant qualifications and experience. For example, including all of your academic achievements, such as your 10th class percentage, 12th class percentage, and your bachelor's degree percentage, may seem impressive, but it's not necessarily relevant to the job you're applying for. In fact, it can actually distract the interviewer from the more important information you want to convey.

It's important to remember that most software development companies care less about your academic percentages and more about your technical skills and experience. In fact, including too much information about your academic performance can make it seem like you're trying to compensate for a lack of technical expertise. Instead of focusing on your academic achievements, you should highlight your relevant technical skills and experience. For example, if you're applying for a software development job, you could highlight your experience with programming languages, databases, and software development methodologies.

When it comes to including academic information in your resume, less is often more. Instead of listing all of your academic achievements in detail, you should focus on your most recent degree and highlight your percentage and year of passing in a single line. This will give the interviewer an idea of your academic background without overwhelming them with unnecessary details. Remember, your resume should be a focused and concise document that highlights your most important qualifications, not a comprehensive account of your entire academic history.

Another reason to avoid including obvious information in your resume is that it can make you seem less professional and less confident. If you're including information that is irrelevant or redundant, it can make it seem like you don't know what's important or that you're trying too hard to impress the interviewer. Instead, you should focus on creating a resume that is clear, concise, and well-organized. This will demonstrate your professionalism and confidence, and make it easier for the interviewer to understand your qualifications and experience.

In addition to avoiding obvious information, there are a few other tips you can follow to create a more effective and impactful resume. First, you should tailor your resume to the specific job you're applying for. This means highlighting the skills and experience that are most relevant to the job, and tailoring your language and formatting to match the requirements of the job description. Second, you should use strong action verbs and clear, concise language to describe your accomplishments and qualifications. This will help to make your resume more engaging and memorable. Finally, you should proofread your resume carefully to ensure that it is free from errors and typos. A well-written and error-free resume will demonstrate your attention to detail and professionalism.

In conclusion, it's important to avoid including obvious information in your resume, such as academic percentages that are irrelevant to the job you're applying for. Instead, you should focus on highlighting your most relevant qualifications and experience, and tailoring your language and formatting to match the requirements of the job. By following these tips, you can create a strong and impactful resume that will help you stand out from the crowd and land the job of your dreams.

CHAPTER FOURTEEN

Avoiding Plagiarism in Your Resume: Tips for Crafting Authentic Content

When it comes to creating a standout resume, it can be tempting to borrow language or content from other sources, whether it's from the internet or from a friend's resume. However, this is a risky move that can ultimately hurt your chances of landing the job you want.

Copying and pasting content from other sources can be a red flag for interviewers, who can quickly spot when language or formatting seems too familiar. This can lead them to doubt your authenticity and creativity, as well as your ability to communicate effectively.

One of the most common areas where plagiarism occurs in resumes is in the "About Me" or mission statement section. Many job seekers turn to the internet to find inspiration for these types of statements, but often end up copying language verbatim or with slight modifications. This can be a major turn-off for interviewers, who want to see that you have put in the effort to craft a unique and compelling message that speaks to your individual strengths and goals.

So how can you avoid plagiarism in your resume? The key is to take inspiration from other sources, rather than copying them outright. Start by gathering a handful of examples of mission statements or other content that you like and that aligns with your goals and values. Use these as a starting point, but then take the time to rewrite them in your own words and voice.

When crafting your mission statement or other content, think about what sets you apart from other candidates and what unique value you can bring to the position. Avoid using buzzwords or generic language that could apply to anyone. Instead, focus on specific accomplishments or experiences that demonstrate your skills and qualifications.

It's also important to ensure that your resume is consistent in style and formatting, and that it reflects your individuality and personality. Don't be afraid to inject some creativity or personality into your writing, but be sure to keep it professional and appropriate for the position you are applying for.

Finally, be sure to proofread your resume carefully and thoroughly, and consider having someone else review it as well. This can help you catch any instances of plagiarism or other errors that could hurt your chances of landing the job.

In conclusion, copying content from other sources is a common mistake that many job seekers make in their resumes. However, this can be a major red flag for interviewers, who want to see that you have put in the effort to craft a unique and authentic message that speaks to your individual strengths and goals. By taking inspiration from other sources and putting in the effort to write your own unique content, you can create a standout resume that will help you land the job you want.

CHAPTER FIFTEEN

The Winning Formula: How to Create a Technical Resume That Lands You the Job

When it comes to applying for a technical job, a well-crafted resume that highlights your technical skills, teamwork, coding projects, leadership, and problem-solving abilities is crucial. Your resume is the first thing that an employer will look at, and it can make or break your chances of getting an interview. Here are some key focus areas to help you create an impressive technical resume:

1. **Technical Skills:**

   Your technical skills are the most important aspect of your resume. The employer wants to know what technical skills you possess and how they can be applied to their company. Make sure to list your technical skills prominently at the top of your resume. This should include programming languages, software and tools that you are proficient in.

2. **Coding Projects:**

Your coding projects are another critical aspect of your resume. It is important to mention any coding projects that you have worked on, including the project title and a brief one-line description. Be careful not to write too much about each project. If an employer is interested, they will ask for more information during the interview. Mention the technologies used in each project, such as the programming languages and frameworks used.

3. **Teamwork:**

   Employers are always looking for team players, so it is important to highlight your teamwork skills on your resume. Make sure to mention the team size of each project that you worked on. If you have never worked on a team, mention any extracurricular activities or volunteer work that involved collaboration with others.

4. **Leadership**:

   Leadership skills are highly valued in the tech industry, so it is important to highlight any leadership roles you have taken on. This could include leading a team on a project, mentoring junior developers, or taking the lead on a challenging task.

5. **Problem Solving:**

   Problem-solving skills are critical for any technical job. Make sure to mention any challenging problems that you have faced and how you solved them. This will show the employer that you have the ability to think critically and come up with solutions to complex problems.

When writing your technical resume, it is essential to avoid overwriting. Stick to the facts and avoid writing lengthy descriptions. Make sure to include only the most relevant information. This will help create a sense of curiosity in the mind of the employer and prompt them to ask you more questions about your projects and your skills.

In conclusion, your technical resume should be focused on your technical skills, teamwork, coding projects, leadership, and problem-solving abilities. Mention at least three coding projects, provide a brief description of each, and make sure to highlight the technologies used. Emphasize your team player and leadership skills, and demonstrate your ability to solve complex problems. Remember to keep your resume concise and avoid overwriting. By following these tips, you can create an impressive technical resume that will help you stand out from the crowd and land your dream job.

CHAPTER SIXTEEN

Sample Resume

Example 1

John Doe 1234 Main Street, Anytown, USA | (555) 555-5555 | john.doe@email.com

Summary:

Highly skilled software development engineer with over 5 years of experience in designing and implementing complex software applications. Proficient in various programming languages and development tools. Adept at working in fast-paced environments and collaborating with cross-functional teams.

Skills:

- Programming languages: Java, Python, C++, JavaScript
- Web development frameworks: React, AngularJS, Node.js
- Databases: MySQL, MongoDB, Oracle
- Development tools: Eclipse, Visual Studio Code, Git, JIRA
- Operating systems: Windows, Linux, MacOS

Experience:

Software Development Engineer, XYZ Corporation January 2019 - Present

• Developed and maintained software applications using Java, Python and React frameworks

• Designed and implemented REST APIs for client-server communication

• Collaborated with cross-functional teams to ensure timely delivery of software products

• Conducted code reviews and mentored junior developers

Software Engineer, ABC Company June 2016 - December 2018

• Developed and maintained software applications using C++ and Python programming languages

• Designed and implemented algorithms for data processing and analysis

• Conducted unit testing and integration testing for software products

• Worked with the team to ensure adherence to coding standards and best practices

Education:

Bachelor of Science in Computer Science, University of XYZ Graduated: May 2016

Certifications:

• Oracle Certified Java Programmer (OCP)

• Microsoft Certified Professional Developer (MCPD)

Projects:

E-commerce website using React framework

• Developed an e-commerce website using React and Node.js frameworks

• Implemented RESTful APIs for product catalog, cart management, and checkout process

• Designed and developed a responsive user interface using Material-UI components

Real-time data processing using Apache Spark

• Implemented a real-time data processing application using Apache Spark

• Designed and developed algorithms for data aggregation and analysis

• Integrated the application with a data streaming platform using Kafka and Spark Streaming

References:

Available upon request.

Example 2:

Name: John Doe Contact Information:

Email: johndoe@email.com

Phone: 555-1234

Summary:

A highly skilled software development engineer with 5+ years of experience in developing web and mobile applications. Proficient in multiple programming languages and frameworks including Java, Python, AngularJS, React Native, and Node.js. Strong problem-solving skills and experience working in Agile development teams.

Skills:

- Programming languages: Java, Python, JavaScript, TypeScript, HTML/CSS
- Frameworks: Spring Boot, Django, AngularJS, React Native, Node.js
- Databases: MySQL, MongoDB, PostgreSQL
- Tools: Git, JIRA, Jenkins, AWS

Experience:

Software Development Engineer ABC Company Jan 2019 - Present

- Developed and maintained web applications using Java, Spring Boot, and MySQL
- Designed and implemented RESTful APIs to connect the front-end and back-end of applications
- Worked in an Agile development team, participating in daily stand-ups, sprint planning, and code reviews

Software Engineer XYZ Corporation May 2016 - Dec 2018

- Worked on a team developing mobile applications using React Native
- Implemented push notifications and location tracking features using native modules
- Participated in regular code reviews and contributed to improving the overall quality of the codebase

Education:

Bachelor of Science in Computer Science University of ABC Graduated May 2016

Example 3:

Name: Jane Smith Contact Information:
Email: janesmith@email.com
Phone: 555-5678

Summary:

A software development engineer with 7+ years of experience in developing enterprise-level applications. Experienced in multiple programming languages including Java, C#, and Python. Strong leadership skills and experience managing development teams.

Skills:

Programming languages: Java, C#, Python, JavaScript
Frameworks: Spring, .NET, AngularJS, React
Databases: Oracle, Microsoft SQL Server, PostgreSQL
Tools: Git, JIRA, Jenkins, Azure, AWS

Experience:

Lead Software Engineer DEF Corporation Oct 2018 - Present

- Led a team of 5 software engineers in the development of a new enterprise-level application using Java and Spring

- Designed and implemented microservices architecture using AWS Lambda and API Gateway
- Participated in Agile development process, leading daily stand-ups and sprint planning

Software Engineer GHI Solutions Jan 2013 - Sept 2018

- Developed web and desktop applications using C# and .NET framework
- Worked with Oracle and Microsoft SQL Server databases
- Participated in code reviews and contributed to improving the quality of the codebase

Education:

Bachelor of Science in Computer Science University of XYZ Graduated May 2012

Example 4:

[Full Name]
[Address]
[Phone Number]
[Email Address]

Career Objective:

To obtain a challenging position as a Software Development Engineer in a reputable organization where I can utilize my technical and interpersonal skills to contribute to the development of innovative software solutions.

Education:

Bachelor of Engineering in Computer Science and Engineering [College/University Name], [Graduation Date] CGPA: [CGPA]

Technical Skills:

Programming Languages: C++, Java, Python Web Development: HTML, CSS, JavaScript, ReactJS Database: MySQL, MongoDB Operating Systems: Windows, Linux Tools: Git, Visual Studio Code, Eclipse

Projects:

[Project Title]

- Developed a web application using ReactJS and NodeJS to manage customer orders for a small business
- Utilized MongoDB to store and retrieve data
- Collaborated with a team of 4 to complete the project within the given timeline

[Project Title]

- Developed a C++ program to perform basic arithmetic operations on matrices
- Implemented error handling to ensure proper input from the user
- Worked independently to design and implement the program

Internships:

[Internship Title], [Company Name], [Duration]

- Worked on developing a mobile application using Java and Android Studio
- Gained experience in software development practices and collaborated with team members

[Internship Title], [Company Name], [Duration]

- Assisted in the development of a web application using HTML, CSS, and JavaScript
- Gained experience in front-end web development and contributed to the project

Achievements:

[Achievement 1]
[Achievement 2]

Extra-Curricular Activities:

[Activity 1]
[Activity 2]

Personal Skills:

- Strong problem-solving skills
- Good communication and interpersonal skills
- Ability to work in a team environment

References:

Available upon request.

Example 5:

John Smith
123 Main Street Anytown,
USA 12345 (555) 555-5555
johnsmith@email.com

Objective:

To obtain a software development engineer position in a dynamic company where I can utilize my skills and experience to contribute to the success of the organization.

Education:

Bachelor of Science in Computer Science, XYZ University, Anytown, USA, May 2017

Skills:

- Proficient in Java, C++, Python, SQL, and other programming languages
- Experience with Agile development methodologies
- Familiarity with web development technologies such as HTML, CSS, and JavaScript
- Strong problem-solving skills
- Excellent communication and teamwork skills

Experience:

Software Developer, ABC Company, Anytown, USA, June 2017 - Present

- Worked on the development of various software applications using Java and Python
- Collaborated with a team of developers and designers to ensure successful project completion
- Assisted in the design and implementation of new features and functionality
- Debugged and fixed issues in existing software applications
- Participated in code reviews and provided feedback to team members

Projects:

- Developed a Java-based chat application for a class project
- Created a Python script to automate data analysis tasks for a research project

Certifications:

Oracle Certified Java Programmer (OCP) - Java SE 8 Programmer Certification

References:

Available upon request.

Rahul Lahoria

CTO

- Building and Leading Teams
- Designing and Building Products
- Project Planning and Risk Management
- Fast MVP and testing Markets
- Planning and Building IPs
- Pulling & Pushing Team Members to reach 300%
- High Resource Optimisation
- Writing Code to Inspire for More
- Solving Coding Challenge for Devs

Contact

Phone
+91-9599075955

Email
rahul_lahoria@yahoo.com

Address
Delhi, India
rahullahoria.com

Education

2014
Master in Technology (M.Tech)
India Institute of Technology (IIT), Kharagpur

Expertise

- **Nodejs**, Python, PHP, Java
- Angular, Reactjs, **React Native**, IONIC, Django
- **Kubernetes, Docker, Cloud tools & computing**
- **MongoDB**, MySQL, **Redis**
- **Building and Leading Teams**
- Creating **Fast MVPS**
- **Building secure, scalable and stable Products**
- **Javascript**, Java, Python, Kotalen, PHP

Language

English
Hindi

Experience

Co-Founder & CTO | Mogi I/O, Delhi, India | *OCT 2018 - Present*
Built Media Tech, Image Optimisation, Video Transcoding, Video Steaming, Video Player Video Compression, CMS, Multi CDN Streaming, VAST & Ad Mob and White Label OTT APP (Web, Android, Android TV, iOS, FireOS, WebOS, TizonOS, tvOS)

Co-Founder & CTO | Livechek, Delhi, India | *SEPT 2017 - OCT 2018*
AI Motor Vehicle inspection App, using AI we were doing dent and scratch detection

Founder & CEO | Shatkon Labs Pvt. Ltd, Delhi, India
OCT 2015 - SEPT 2017
Smart Public Advertisement System, digital billboard ads could be shown based on people around it.

SDE | Capillary Technologies, Bangalore, India
JUN 2014 - OCT 2015
Built User Data Centralisation System, Cloud Resource Management Portal

Patents

SYSTEM AND METHOD FOR TRANSFERRING DATA PACKETS OVER NETWORK SECURELY
(15082) 201911040414-DEL with Cutting Edge Digital Pvt. Ltd., Delhi, India
A method for enhancing rate of transfer of data packets over network

SYSTEM TO DETERMINE MAGNETIC HEADING OF A MOBILE DEVICE
(15082) TEMP/E- 1/23294/2018-DEL with LiveChek Pvt. Ltd., Delhi, India
To get right direction of from which photograph is taken

SYSTEM AND METHOD FOR STEP DETECTION USING A MOBILE DEVICE
(15082) TEMP/E- 1/23281/2018-DEL with LiveChek Pvt. Ltd., Delhi, india
To get more correct step taken from start to end. When mobile phone is in hand of use with fist movement

METHOD AND SYSTEM FOR DETERMINING LOCATION OF A USER HOLDING A MOBILE DEVICE *(15082) TEMP/E- 1/23308/2018-DEL*

TIME INTERLEAVED DIGITAL TRANSMITTER USING MULTI LEVEL DIGITAL QUANTIZATION
(15082) TEMP/E- 1/23268/2018-DEL

COMPUTING SYSTEM FOR RUNNING COMPUTATIONALLY INTENSIVE SOFTWARE APPLICATION IN COMPUTING DEVICE HAVING LIMITED COMPUTATIONAL RESOURCE
(9344) 832/KOL/2014

Reference

Ra
Phone:
Email:

Pi
Phone:
Email:

My Sample Resume: Build by Canva

Enhancing Your Resume with Design Tools: Tips and Tricks

In today's job market, it's not just about having the right skills and experience, it's also about presenting yourself in the best possible light. This is where the design and aesthetics of your resume come into play. A well-designed resume not only helps you stand out from the crowd, but it also showcases your attention to detail and creativity.

One of the easiest ways to create a visually appealing resume is by using design tools such as Canva. Canva is a free online graphic design tool that allows you to create stunning visuals, including resumes, with ease.

Before you start designing your resume, it's important to identify the key sections that should be included. These sections typically include a professional summary or objective statement, work experience, education, skills, and any relevant certifications or awards.

Once you have identified these sections, it's time to start designing. Canva offers a wide variety of templates specifically designed for resumes. You can select a template that suits your needs and customize it with your own personal information, colors, and font styles.

When designing your resume, it's important to keep it simple and easy to read. Avoid using too many colors or fonts, as this can make your resume look cluttered and difficult to follow. Stick to a few colors and fonts that complement each other and are easy on the eyes.

Another tip when using design tools is to use icons and images to break up the text and make your resume more visually appealing. You can use icons to represent different skills or sections of your resume, and images to showcase any work you have done or awards you have received.

In conclusion, using design tools such as Canva can help you create a visually appealing and professional resume that showcases your skills and experience. Remember to keep it simple, use a few complementary colors and fonts, and use icons and images to make your resume stand out. With a well-designed resume, you'll be one step closer to landing your dream job.

CHAPTER SEVENTEEN

Effective Strategies for Reaching Key People in a Company for Job Opportunities

In today's fast-paced job market, finding the right job can be a challenging task. With numerous job portals available, it can be difficult to stand out and get noticed by potential employers. However, there are alternative ways to reach key people within a company, and this can help you land your dream job. In this article, we will discuss the importance of reaching key people within a company and how to do it effectively.

Traditional job portals such as Naukri, Monster, and Indeed have long been the go-to platforms for job seekers. However, due to their popularity, these portals have become overcrowded, and it is difficult to stand out among the sea of resumes. To make matters worse, the companies and HR agencies that use these portals are often overwhelmed with resumes, making it difficult for them to identify the right candidates. As a result, getting a job interview call from these portals can be a daunting task.

Fortunately, there are alternative ways to reach potential employers. One such method is through LinkedIn and the company's website. LinkedIn is a professional networking site that connects professionals from all over the world. By leveraging LinkedIn, job seekers can reach out to key people within a company and showcase their skills and experience.

The first step in reaching out to key people within a company is to create a write-up. The write-up should be concise and compelling. In the first paragraph, you should talk about what you like about the company. This can be something as simple as their mission or values. In the second paragraph, you should express your excitement about working with them. This can be a great opportunity to show your enthusiasm for the company and the role you are interested in. In the third paragraph, you should highlight your skills and experience. Be sure to tailor this section to the specific role you are applying for. You can also attach your resume to the write-up, making it easy for potential employers to review your qualifications.

When reaching out to key people within a company, it is important to identify who those key people are. HR, team leads, CTOs, and CEOs are often the decision-makers when it comes to hiring. These individuals have the power to hire you or refer you to the right person. Sending your write-up to these individuals can increase your chances of getting noticed and landing an interview.

Once you have identified the key people within a company, you can reach out to them through email or LinkedIn messages. To find their email address, visit the company's website and look for the "contact us" or "about us" section. From there, you can typically find the email addresses of key people within the company. If you're reaching out through LinkedIn, you can send a direct message to the individual you want to connect with.

It's important to note that reaching out to key people within a company takes time and effort. It's not something that can be done in a day or two. A good strategy is to spend an hour each day identifying four companies that you're interested in and connecting with the key people within those companies. This can help you build a network of contacts and increase your chances of getting noticed.

Reaching out to key people within a company can be a great way to land your dream job. However, it's important to approach this method with the right mindset. You should not expect immediate results, and it may take some time to hear back from potential employers. The key is to remain persistent and to keep reaching out to potential employers until you get the job you want.

In conclusion, reaching out to key people within a company can be an effective way to get noticed and land your dream job. By leveraging LinkedIn and the company's website, you can connect with decision-makers and showcase your skills and experience. Remember to be persistent and patient, and don't give up.

Example 1:

Dear [Hiring Manager's Name],

I am a recent graduate with a degree in Computer Science and a strong passion for software development. I am excited to apply for the Software Development Engineer position at [Company Name], as it aligns with my skills and interests.

During my studies, I gained experience in several programming languages, including Java, Python, and C++. I also worked on various projects, such as developing a web-based application using Django and creating a database management system using MySQL. Additionally, I have experience working with version control tools such as Git and using Agile methodology in team projects.

I am confident that my skills and experience would make me an asset to your team. I am highly motivated to learn and grow in a fast-paced environment and I believe that [Company Name] would be a great place for me to achieve my professional goals.

Thank you for considering my application. I would be honored to discuss further how my qualifications and experience would benefit your organization.

Best regards, [Your Name]

Example 2:

Hello [Hiring Manager's Name],

I hope this message finds you well. I am reaching out to express my interest in the software development engineer position at [Company Name]. As a recent computer science graduate, I am excited to apply my skills and knowledge to a challenging role in a dynamic company like yours.

Throughout my studies, I have developed a strong foundation in programming languages such as Java, Python, and C++, and have worked on various projects that involved creating web applications, mobile apps, and game development. I am also familiar with agile methodologies and have experience working in a team environment.

I am eager to learn from experienced professionals and contribute to the company's success. I believe that my technical skills, passion for software development, and enthusiasm for learning make me a great fit for the role.

Please find my attached resume for your consideration. I look forward to hearing back from you soon.

Best regards,

[Your Name]

Example 3:

Dear [Hiring Manager's Name],

I am writing to express my interest in the software development engineer role at [Company Name]. As a recent computer science graduate, I have a strong foundation in programming languages and am eager to apply my skills to a challenging role in a dynamic organization.

Throughout my studies, I have gained experience in programming languages such as Java, Python, and C++, and have worked on various projects including creating web applications and mobile apps. I have also collaborated with my peers on group projects and have experience using agile methodologies.

I am excited about the opportunity to work with experienced professionals and to learn and grow in a dynamic work environment. I am confident that my technical skills, passion for software development, and willingness to learn make me a great fit for the role.

Please find my resume attached for your review. Thank you for considering my application. I look forward to the opportunity to discuss my candidacy further.

Sincerely,
[Your Name]

Following the successful completion of the previous steps, you are now prepared to perform well during your job interview. In the next section, we will discuss some tips and strategies on how to ace your interview.

CHAPTER EIGHTEEN

From Blank Page to Successful Career: A Comprehensive Guide for Freshers on Resume Building and Reaching Out

As a fresher, building a strong resume and networking with people is crucial for landing a good job. Here are 10 key points to focus on while building a resume and reaching out to people:

1. **Highlight Relevant Skills:**

   As a fresher, you may not have much work experience, but you can highlight your relevant skills in your resume. List your technical skills and mention any projects you have worked on. Make sure to mention any extracurricular activities or leadership roles you have taken on.

2. **Customize your Resume for Each Job:**

   One-size-fits-all resumes are not effective. Customize your

resume for each job application by highlighting the skills and experiences that match the job requirements.

3. **Use Keywords:**

   Many companies use applicant tracking systems (ATS) to filter resumes. To ensure your resume passes the ATS, use keywords related to the job in your resume. Analyze the job description and use the same keywords in your resume.

4. **Include a Cover Letter:**

   A well-written cover letter can make your application stand out. Use it to highlight your skills, experiences, and interest in the job. Make sure to customize your cover letter for each job application.

5. **Create a LinkedIn Profile:**

   LinkedIn is a professional networking platform. Create a LinkedIn profile and make sure to include your education, skills, and experiences. Connect with people in your field and participate in LinkedIn groups to network with professionals.

6. **Attend Networking Events:**

   Attend job fairs, conferences, and networking events to meet professionals in your field. Prepare a 30-second elevator pitch that highlights your skills and experiences.

7. **Leverage Your Network:**

   Reach out to your professors, alumni, and peers for advice and referrals. Many jobs are filled through referrals, so it's important to build a strong network.

8. **Build an Online Presence:**

   Employers often search for candidates online. Build an online presence by creating a personal website or blog that showcases your skills and experiences.

9. **Get Involved in Open Source Projects:**

   Contributing to open-source projects is a great way to gain real-world experience and showcase your skills to potential employers.

10. **Practice for Interviews:**

    Prepare for interviews by practicing common interview questions and participating in mock interviews. Research the company and prepare questions to ask during the interview.

By focusing on these key points, you can build a strong resume, create a professional network, and increase your chances of landing a good job as a fresher. Remember to stay positive, persistent, and keep refining your skills and experiences.

CHAPTER NINETEEN

Part 2: Summary

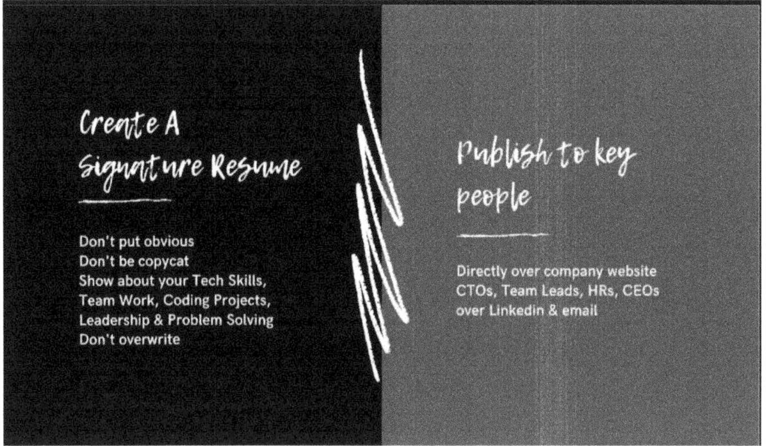

2 steps for getting interview calls

3rd P : Perform (How to give best interview)

An awesome interview is not just about showing off your skills, but about connecting with your interviewer, demonstrating your passion, and leaving a lasting impression that sets you apart from the rest

CHAPTER TWENTY

The One-Month Wonder: A Tale of Unexpected Success

It was a cold November morning in 2014 when I woke up at 7 AM, just like any other day. However, this particular day was different. I had given a test for an interview inside two companies, and I discovered that I had made it to the next round for both of them. The first company was a Japanese corporation that was offering a decent salary, while the other was a seven-year-old startup called Capillary Technology that was also paying well. Despite the financial aspect, I was more excited about Capillary Technology.

However, I was also nervous because I only had one month to prepare for the interviews, whereas most of my peers had been preparing for over six months. One friend of mine, Arun, had been preparing for just as long and had gone through every available online and offline resource to be as prepared as possible. I was intimidated by his dedication and knowledge as I only had one month to prepare, focusing on Stack, DSA, and DBMS.

In the first round, thousands of students had applied, but only one hundred students were selected for the second round, and I was one of them. However, I was more concerned about Arun than the other ninety-eight students who did not make it to the next round.

The second round was a handwritten code test where we were given two problems to solve. The first one involved creating a solution to evaluate a sudoku solution, while the second one dealt with a circular buffer. Out of the hundred students, only twenty qualified for the third round, and fortunately, Arun and I were among them.

As we progressed through the rounds, the competition became tougher, and I was increasingly nervous about Arun, who had put in so much hard work and dedication. In the fourth round, only ten students were selected, and both Arun and I made the cut. Then, we both made it to the final fifth round, where we had to give our best to secure a job.

When the results were announced, I was thrilled to learn that I had been selected for the position, but I was also shocked that Arun had failed. I couldn't help but wonder what had gone wrong, given that Arun was well-versed in all the concepts and had dedicated so much time to preparing for the interview.

This incident sparked my curiosity, and I decided to investigate what had happened differently. I spent time analyzing the factors that might have contributed to Arun's failure and compared them to my success.

Then I found following 7 things

You have prepared for the interview, you have also published your resume and now you have the interview to give. So if you give your interview in a correct way it will increase your chance to getting selected by 70%.

CHAPTER TWENTY-ONE

Mastering the Art of Ambiguity: Why Asking Questions in Interviews Can Make or Break Your Chances of Success

The Importance of Avoiding Assumptions in Job Interviews

Job interviews can be nerve-wracking experiences for many individuals, and the pressure to perform well can lead to making assumptions about the interview questions or the expectations of the interviewer. However, making assumptions can often lead to misunderstandings and mistakes, potentially jeopardizing the chances of getting selected for the job.

As humans, we often have a habit of assuming things, and it is important to recognize this tendency when preparing for a job interview. It is also possible that we might have encountered similar problems or questions before, which can further reinforce our assumptions. In either scenario, it is crucial to ensure that we avoid making any assumptions during the interview process.

One of the best ways to avoid making assumptions is by clarifying any ambiguities within the problem. Whenever you come across a question or problem that is not clear, it is important to ask the interviewer for clarification. Doing so demonstrates that you understand the problem and that you recognize the presence of any ambiguity. It also shows that you are willing to take the time to clarify any misunderstandings, which can increase your chances of getting selected.

By asking questions, you can also build up a conversation with the interviewer. This is beneficial because it helps you establish a rapport with the interviewer, which can put you at ease and create a more relaxed atmosphere. Building up the conversation also demonstrates your interest in the company and the role you are applying for, which can leave a positive impression on the interviewer.

Finally, clarifying ambiguities can give the interviewer the impression that the problem is new to you. This is an opportunity to showcase your problem-solving abilities and demonstrate your capacity to learn quickly. As you provide a correct answer to the problem, it can leave a lasting impression on the interviewer, increasing your chances of getting selected.

In conclusion, avoiding assumptions during job interviews is critical for success. Clarifying ambiguities demonstrates your ability to understand the problem and your willingness to seek clarification. By doing so, you can establish a rapport with the interviewer, create a positive impression, and demonstrate your problem-solving abilities. By recognizing the tendency to assume and taking steps to avoid it, you can increase your chances of success in job interviews.

Here are 10 scenarios at a coding interview where a candidate may need to ask questions:

1. Sarah was asked to write a program that calculates the total cost of items in a shopping cart. However, she wasn't sure if she should include taxes in the calculation or not. To clarify this, she asked the interviewer if taxes should be included in the calculation.
2. John was given a question that involved creating a search algorithm. He wasn't sure if the search was case-sensitive or not. He asked the interviewer if the search was case-sensitive or if it was case-insensitive.
3. Lisa was given a problem that involved working with a database. However, the interviewer did not specify which type of database should be used. Lisa asked the interviewer if there were any specific databases that she should use or if she could use any database of her choice.

4. Tom was given a question that required him to work with APIs. He was unsure which APIs to use and how to use them. He asked the interviewer for more information on which APIs to use and how to use them.

5. Kate was given a problem that involved working with data structures. However, she was unsure which data structure to use for the given problem. She asked the interviewer for advice on which data structure would be the best fit for the problem.

6. David was asked to create a program that involved working with time zones. However, he wasn't sure how to handle time zones in different regions. He asked the interviewer for guidance on how to handle time zones in different regions.

7. Jessica was given a problem that required her to create a user interface. However, she was unsure which programming language to use to create the user interface. She asked the interviewer if there were any restrictions on which programming language she could use.

8. James was asked to create a program that involved working with files. However, he wasn't sure if he should create a new file or work with an existing one. He asked the interviewer if he should create a new file or work with an existing one.

9. Sarah was given a question that involved working with machine learning algorithms. However, she was unsure which algorithm to use for the given problem. She asked the interviewer for advice on which machine learning algorithm would be the best fit for the problem.

10. Mike was asked to create a program that involved working with encryption. However, he was unsure which encryption algorithm to use. He asked the interviewer for guidance on which encryption algorithm would be the best fit for the problem.

CHAPTER TWENTY-TWO

The Art of Pretending: How to Ace Your Coding Interview

When it comes to coding interviews, it's common to have a lot of nerves and pressure to perform well. However, even in the midst of stress, it's important to demonstrate to the interviewer that you are capable of approaching a problem from scratch, and that you have the ability to communicate your thought process clearly.

> "*Sometime it can happen you already know the solution of the problem, at that time also you should make cuttings inside your solution. This shows to the interviewer you are creating the solution at that time only.*"

One of the most important things to keep in mind during a coding interview is to avoid the temptation to rely on preexisting solutions that you've memorized or practiced beforehand. Even if you happen to have a solution in mind that matches the problem, it's essential to show your work and demonstrate how you arrived at the solution. This not only helps to build your credibility as a problem solver, but it also gives the interviewer an opportunity to assess your thought process.

One technique to help with this is to "make cuttings" in your solution. Essentially, this means breaking down your solution into smaller steps and only writing down the key parts of each step. This shows the interviewer that you're not simply reciting a solution that you've memorized, but rather that you're actively working through the problem in real time.

It's also important to go through all phases of problem solving, including designing your solution, conversing with the interviewer, writing your code, and testing your solution. This demonstrates that you have a well-rounded approach to problem solving and that you're not simply rushing to write code without properly considering the problem at hand.

Additionally, it's important to communicate your thought process to the interviewer throughout the process. This helps the interviewer understand how you're approaching the problem and gives them an opportunity to guide you if needed. By doing this, you also demonstrate that you're capable of working collaboratively and taking feedback.

In conclusion, during a coding interview, it's important to demonstrate your ability to work through a problem from scratch, rather than relying on memorized solutions. Making cuttings in your solution, going through all phases of problem solving, and communicating your thought process clearly to the interviewer can all help to showcase your skills as a problem solver and increase your chances of success.

CHAPTER TWENTY-THREE

Don't Guess: When to Admit You're Not Sure

Guessing is a tempting option when you are faced with a coding problem that you don't know the solution to. However, it is crucial to remember that guessing incorrectly can have a detrimental impact on your chances of getting selected in a coding interview. Here are some dos and don'ts to keep in mind when faced with a problem you are unsure about.

Firstly, if you have a vague idea about a solution but are not sure, it's better to communicate that to the interviewer. A good approach is to say "as best I can remember, this should be the answer." This approach proactively tells the interviewer that you are not 100% confident about your answer. If your guess happens to be right, it shows that you have some knowledge about the topic. On the other hand, if your guess is wrong, the interviewer won't count it against you as you have already stated your uncertainty.

However, it is essential to keep in mind that guessing should not be your go-to strategy. If you find yourself guessing more than 30% of the time, it is a red flag that you need to improve your preparation. In such cases, it is better to be upfront with the interviewer and say, "I'm not entirely sure about the answer. Would you like me to give it a try?" This approach shows that you are willing to give it a shot, but at the same time, you are not overconfident.

It is also essential to learn from your guesses and clarify those questions in your preparation for the next interview. This approach helps to decrease your chances of getting rejected in your next coding interview.

In conclusion, guessing is not a bad strategy in coding interviews, as long as it is used sparingly and in the right way. It is important to communicate your uncertainty to the interviewer and not rely too heavily on guesses. Remember, guessing is a valuable tool in your arsenal, but it should not be your only one.

CHAPTER TWENTY-FOUR

From Worst to Best: The Art of Presenting Multiple Solutions in a Coding Interview

In the field of computer science, problem-solving and algorithm design are crucial skills for any programmer or software engineer. Often during interviews, candidates are asked to solve a particular problem or implement an algorithm for a given task. However, for every problem, there can be multiple solutions, each with its own advantages and disadvantages.

Knowing multiple solutions to a problem is certainly an advantage, but it is equally important to know how to present them during an interview. In many cases, it is not enough to provide just one solution to a problem, especially if it is not optimal. Therefore, a candidate should be prepared to present multiple solutions, starting with the worst one.

The reason for this is simple: interviewers are not only interested in the final solution but also in the thought process that goes into finding it. By presenting the worst solution first, candidates can demonstrate their analytical and critical thinking skills, as well as their ability to identify and acknowledge weaknesses in their approach.

Moreover, presenting multiple solutions allows interviewers to gain insight into a candidate's problem-solving skills, as they can see how a candidate iteratively improves upon their solutions, eventually arriving at the optimal one.

Another reason to start with the worst solution is that it can help build rapport with the interviewer. Presenting a suboptimal solution first can make the candidate appear humble and honest, which can create a positive impression on the interviewer.

However, it is important to note that presenting a bad solution should not be an excuse to present a completely unworkable or incorrect solution. Rather, the candidate should present a solution that is technically correct but inefficient or has other issues.

Once the candidate presents the worst solution, the interviewer may ask how it can be improved. This is the perfect opportunity for the candidate to demonstrate their problem-solving skills by proposing an alternative, more efficient solution. Ideally, this solution should be better than the previous one but still not optimal.

The process of presenting multiple solutions and improving upon them should continue until the candidate arrives at the optimal solution. The solutions can be presented in increasing order of complexity or decreasing order of time complexity.

For example, if the problem involves sorting a list of integers, a candidate can start by presenting a solution that involves iterating over the list and swapping elements, resulting in a time complexity of O(n^2). The interviewer may then ask if there is a more efficient way to sort the list, to which the candidate can present an algorithm such as quicksort or mergesort, which have a time complexity of O(nlogn). If the interviewer is still not satisfied, the candidate can propose other solutions such as radix sort or counting sort, which have a time complexity of O(n) or O(n+k), respectively.

It is important to note that the process of presenting multiple solutions should not be rushed. Candidates should take the time to explain each solution thoroughly, including its strengths and weaknesses. They should also be prepared to answer any questions the interviewer may have about the solutions.

Additionally, candidates should not feel discouraged if they cannot arrive at the optimal solution right away. It is common for candidates to struggle with some problems, and interviewers understand that. The key is to show a willingness to learn and improve, as well as the ability to think critically and creatively.

In summary, presenting multiple solutions to a problem during an interview can be a great way to demonstrate one's problem-solving skills and critical thinking abilities. Starting with the worst solution and iterating towards the optimal one can also help build rapport with the interviewer and create a positive impression. However, candidates should take the time to explain each solution thoroughly and be prepared to answer any questions the interviewer may have.

here are 8 coding questions with solutions ranging from O(n^2) to O(log(n)) time complexity:

1. Find the two numbers in an array that add up to a target sum.

a. O(n^2) solution: Iterate through all possible pairs of numbers in the array and check if their sum equals the target.

b. O(nlogn) solution: Sort the array, then use two pointers to scan from both ends towards the middle, checking the sum of the values at each pointer until the target is found or no such pair exists.

c. O(n) solution: Use a hash table to store each number in the array and its index. For each number in the array, check if the difference between the target and the current number is in the hash table.

2. Check if a given string is a palindrome.

a. O(n^2) solution: Iterate through all possible pairs of characters in the string and check if they form a palindrome.

b. O(n) solution: Use two pointers to scan from both ends towards the middle of the string, checking if the characters at each pointer match until the entire string has been checked.

3. Find the maximum subarray sum in an array.

a. O(n^2) solution: Iterate through all possible subarrays in the array and calculate their sum, returning the maximum sum.

b. O(n) solution: Use Kadane's algorithm to find the maximum subarray sum in a single pass through the array.

4. Find the kth largest element in an unsorted array.

a. O(n^2) solution: Use selection sort to sort the array in descending order, then return the kth element.

b. O(nlogn) solution: Use quicksort to sort the array, then return the kth element.

c. O(n) solution: Use the quickselect algorithm, which is similar to quicksort but only sorts the portion of the array containing the kth element.

5. Find all pairs of elements in an array whose product is a given target value.

a. O(n^2) solution: Iterate through all possible pairs of elements in the array and check if their product equals the target.

b. O(nlogn) solution: Sort the array, then use two pointers to scan from both ends towards the middle, checking the product of the values at each pointer until all pairs have been found.

c. O(n) solution: Use a hash table to store each number in the array and its index. For each number in the array, check if the target divided by the current number is in the hash table.

6. Find the peak element in an array (an element that is greater than both of its neighbors).

a. O(n^2) solution: Iterate through all elements in the array and check if each one is a peak element by comparing it to its neighbors.

b. O(n) solution: Use a modified binary search algorithm to find a peak element in the array.

7. Find the first non-repeating character in a string.

a. O(n^2) solution: Iterate through all characters in the string and check if each one appears only once.

b. O(n) solution: Use a hash table to store the frequency of each character in the string, then iterate through the string again to find the first character with a frequency of 1.

8. Determine if a given number is a power of two.

O(logn) solution: Keep dividing the number by 2 until it becomes 1 (or less than 1), checking at each step if the remainder is 0.

O(1) solution: Use bitwise operations to check if the number is a power of two.

CHAPTER TWENTY-FIVE

Why Asking Questions at the End of an Interview can be Crucial for your Job Hunt

As a job seeker, when you are invited for an interview, it is important to prepare yourself adequately in order to make a good impression. One aspect of the interview that many candidates overlook is the opportunity to ask questions at the end of the interview. This is a crucial opportunity for you to show that you are interested in the company and that you have done your research.

Asking questions about the company at the end of an interview can be beneficial in many ways. Firstly, it shows the interviewer that you are interested in the company beyond just getting a job. This can make you stand out from other candidates who may not have asked any questions. Additionally, asking questions can help you gain a better understanding of the company's culture, values, and goals, which can help you decide if this is the right company for you.

Before the interview, take some time to research the company. Go to their website and read about their products, services, and mission statement. Look for news articles or press releases about the company, and take note of any recent developments or achievements. This will help you come up with thoughtful questions that show you have done your research and are genuinely interested in the company.

Here are some examples of questions you can ask at the end of an interview:

1. **What are the company's long-term goals?**

   Asking this question can help you understand the company's direction and plans for the future. It can also give you an idea of where you could fit in and contribute to the company's growth.

2. **How does the company measure success?**

   This question can help you understand what metrics the company values and what kind of goals they set for themselves. It can also help you understand what kind of performance expectations you would be held to.

3. **What kind of training or professional development opportunities are available?**

   Asking about training and professional development opportunities can show that you are interested in continuing to grow and learn in your role. It can also help you decide if the company is invested in the growth and development of its employees.

4. **How does the company approach innovation?**

   Asking this question can help you understand how the company approaches new ideas and technologies. It can also give you an idea of what kind of innovation you could be involved in if you were to join the company.

5. **What is the company culture like?**

   Asking about company culture can help you understand the work environment and what kind of values are important to the company. It can also give you an idea of whether the company would be a good fit for you personally.

6. **How does the company prioritize work-life balance?**

   Asking about work-life balance can show that you value a healthy work-life balance and are looking for a company that prioritizes it as well. It can also help you decide if the company's expectations align with your own.

7. **What are the company's biggest challenges right now?**

   Asking about challenges the company is facing can help you understand the company's pain points and where you could potentially make a difference. It can also give you an idea of what kind of challenges you would be expected to tackle if you were to join the company.

8. **How does the company approach diversity and inclusion?**

   Asking about diversity and inclusion can show that you are interested in working for a company that values diversity and treats all employees fairly. It can also give you an idea of the company's commitment to creating an inclusive workplace.

9. **How does the company give back to the community?**

   Asking about the company's community involvement can help you understand the company's values and commitment to social responsibility. It can also give you an idea of what kind of volunteer or community service opportunities might be available to you as an employee.

10. **What sets this company apart from its competitors?**

    Asking this question can help you understand what makes the company unique.

CHAPTER TWENTY-SIX

Don't Ask about the Salary: Why Asking About Salary Can Cost You the Job

Job interviews can be nerve-wracking experiences, especially if you're desperate for the job. It's natural to want to know what kind of salary you can expect if you're offered the position. However, asking about salary during the interview can send the wrong message to the interviewer. It makes you seem money-minded and uncommitted. In this article, we'll discuss why it's best to avoid salary discussions during the interview process and why honesty and smartness are critical to your interview success.

Firstly, let's understand why asking about salary during the interview can be harmful to your chances of getting the job. Interviewers expect that you are primarily interested in the job itself and the opportunity to work with the company, rather than just the money. When you ask about the salary, it sends a message that you're more interested in how much you can make than in the job itself. It can give the impression that you're not genuinely interested in the position and may not be a committed employee.

Moreover, the salary range for a job can depend on many factors, including experience, qualifications, and market conditions. It's impossible to determine the precise salary that a candidate should receive without considering these factors. Usually, the interviewer or the hiring manager will discuss salary with the selected candidate after they have extended an offer letter. At that time, they may ask for your salary expectations, which will provide you with an opportunity to negotiate.

It's essential to remember that your interview performance can make or break your chances of getting hired. Even if you're well-qualified for the job, a bad interview can end your candidacy. According to research, 70% of job candidates are rejected because of their performance in the interview. So, it's crucial to prepare thoroughly and present yourself in the best possible light during the interview process.

To increase your chances of success in an interview, you must be truthful and smart. This means being honest about your skills, experience, and qualifications, and not exaggerating your abilities or achievements. It also means being smart about how you present yourself and your achievements, highlighting those that are most relevant to the position you're interviewing for.

Here are some tips on how to be smart and truthful during an interview:

1. Be honest about your qualifications and experience. Don't exaggerate your abilities or achievements, as it can come across as insincere.

2. Be prepared to discuss your strengths and weaknesses. Don't try to hide your weaknesses, as this can make you appear dishonest.

3. Be specific when discussing your accomplishments. Don't speak in general terms, but provide specific examples of your achievements that are relevant to the position.

4. Research the company and the position before the interview. This will show the interviewer that you're genuinely interested

in the job.

5. Be prepared to answer common interview questions, such as "why do you want this job?" or "what are your career goals?"

In conclusion, asking about salary during the interview can send the wrong message to the interviewer, making you seem money-minded and uncommitted. It's better to wait until you receive an offer letter to discuss salary or negotiate. Your interview performance can make or break your chances of getting hired, so it's essential to prepare thoroughly and be honest and smart during the interview process. Remember, being truthful and smart can increase your chances of getting selected by at least 50% or more.

CHAPTER TWENTY-SEVEN

The Art of Communication: 10 Key Points for a Fresher to Excel in Coding Interviews

10 key points for a fresher to perform better in coding interviews regarding communication:

1. **Be confident and clear in your communication:** Communication is key in any interview, and being confident and clear in your communication is essential. Speak slowly and clearly, and make sure you are understood by the interviewer.

2. **Listen carefully to the question:** It's important to listen carefully to the question being asked and make sure you understand it fully. Take a moment to think about the question before answering and make sure you answer the question that was asked.

3. **Ask questions for clarification:** If you are unsure about the question or need more information to answer it, don't hesitate to ask the interviewer for clarification. This shows that you are engaged in the conversation and are committed to

understanding the problem.

4. **Think aloud:** When you are solving a coding problem, it's important to think aloud so that the interviewer can understand your thought process. Explain the steps you are taking and why you are taking them, as this will give the interviewer insight into your problem-solving abilities.

5. **Use visual aids:** If you need to explain a complex idea or concept, consider using visual aids like diagrams or flowcharts to help illustrate your point. This can be especially useful in technical interviews where complex algorithms or data structures are being discussed.

6. **Be concise:** While it's important to be clear in your communication, it's also important to be concise. Stick to the point and avoid rambling or going off on tangents. This will help you to communicate your ideas more effectively and avoid confusion.

7. **Practice active listening:** In addition to being clear in your own communication, it's important to practice active listening. This means being fully engaged in the conversation and paying attention to what the interviewer is saying. Show that you are listening by nodding your head, asking follow-up questions, and responding appropriately.

8. **Show enthusiasm and passion:** Employers want to hire candidates who are passionate about their work and enthusiastic about solving problems. Show your enthusiasm and passion by asking thoughtful questions, sharing your own ideas and experiences, and demonstrating your commitment to learning and growing.

9. **Be humble:** While it's important to demonstrate your skills and expertise, it's also important to be humble. Avoid arrogance or overconfidence, and show that you are open to feedback and willing to learn from others.

10. **Follow up after the interview:** After the interview, follow up with the interviewer to thank them for their time and reiterate your interest in the position. This shows that you are serious about the job and committed to making a good impression.

In summary, effective communication is essential in coding interviews, and by being confident, clear, and concise in your communication, listening actively, demonstrating enthusiasm and passion, and following up after the interview, you can increase your chances of performing better in coding interviews.

CHAPTER TWENTY-EIGHT

Part 3: Summary

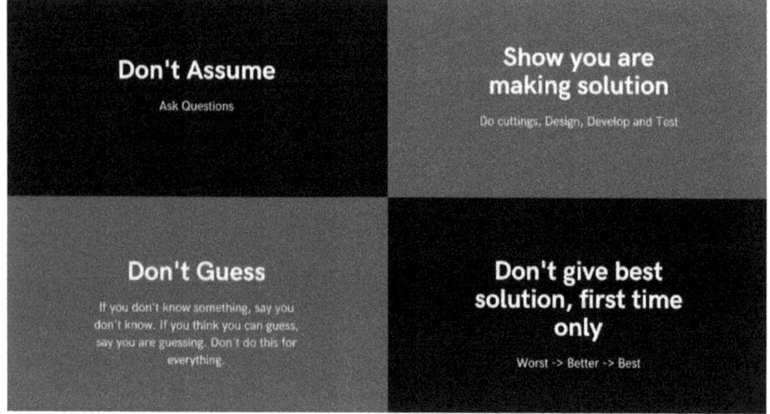

First 4 Key Points

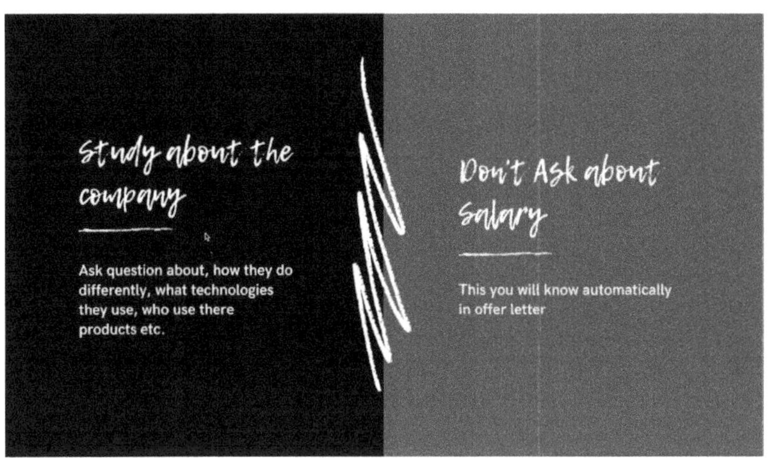

Don't forget these 2 things

Additional Resources

If you're looking to become a ProCoder and crack your next coding interview, make sure to follow me for updates and supporting material on my journey! You can stay up-to-date with my latest tips and resources by following me on my website, Udemy, LinkedIn, Instagram, and even through email. Here are my links for you to follow:

- Website: rahullahoria.com
- Udemy: https://www.udemy.com/user/rahul-lahoria/
- LinkedIn: https://in.linkedin.com/in/rahul-lahoria-36243993
- Instagram: https://www.instagram.com/rahullahoria007/
- Email: rahul_lahoria@yahoo.com

Together, we can work towards achieving your coding goals!

www.ingramcontent.com/pod-product-compliance
Ingram Content Group UK Ltd.
Pitfield, Milton Keynes, MK11 3LW, UK
UKHW022003190726
13853UKWH00004B/1699

9 798890 263230